Cybersecurity: Home and Small Business

Cybersecurity: Home and Small Business

Raef Meeuwisse

Cyber Simplicity Ltd

2016

Raef Meeuwisse, Cyber Simplicity Ltd, Hythe, KENT, UK CT21 5HE.

Email:	orders@cybersimplicity.com
Twitter:	@grcarchitect
First Printing:	2016
ISBN	978-1-911452-04-1
First published by:	Cyber Simplicity Ltd
Edition Date:	6th June 2016

www.cybersimplicity.com

www.cybersecurityhomeandsmallbusiness.com

Ordering Information:

Special discounts are available on quantity purchases by corporations, associations, educators, and others. For details, contact the publisher at the above listed address. Trade bookstores and wholesalers: Please contact Cyber Simplicity Ltd.

Tel/Fax: +44(0)1227 540 540 or email orders@cybersimplicity.com.

For those who have ever been attacked,

For those who do not want to be successfully attacked;

Here is how to minimize the future risks and consequences.

Disclaimer:

This book is designed to provide general security guidance that can help to reduce the risk of being compromised by a cyber attack and more easily recover if one takes place. Security is never impenetrable. Risks, threats and controls are continually evolving. This book is for guidance only and no warranty or guarantee is inferred or implied.

www

the world wild west

Also Available

Also available from this author in paperback & digital formats:

Cybersecurity for Beginners

This book provides an easy insight into the full discipline of cybersecurity, even if you have a non-technical background.

The Cybersecurity to English Dictionary

This book is designed to be a useful companion for anyone who wants to keep up on cybersecurity terms or confound others with their understanding. Finally, cybersecurity does not need to sound like a different language.

The Encrypted Book of Passwords

Writing your passwords down is usually fraught with risks. The encrypted book of passwords helps you to store your passwords more securely in a format that you can read but others will find hard to break.

Visit www.cybersimplicity.com for a full list of the latest titles

.

Looking for great corporate promotional gifts?

Check out our offers at **www.cybersimplicity.com**

Contents

Foreword by Ed Moyle

When I met Raef the first time, what most struck me about him was his passion. One would of course expect an author -- particularly such a prolific one – to have a certain "gusto" for his or her chosen subject matter. And, no exception to this rule, Raef absolutely does. But the passion I'm referring to – what I noticed during my first discussions with him and so many times since - is of a different kind entirely. I'm referring to his innate drive to share his "hard-won" knowledge with others.

As I've grown to know Raef – first as acquaintances and now as friends – I've discovered that his desire to help others and his need to "give back" is a fundamental part of his character. To hoard his expertise or to be miserly with his experience and insights just isn't in his nature. Whereas other professionals might become cynical or jaded -- their faith in humankind eroded by the ocean of fraud, abuse, and criminality that is the battleground of the security practitioner – Raef's optimism, passion, and patience never waver.

Because of this, I cannot think of a more natural or logical choice to help the home user or small business in tackling the tough challenges of cybersecurity. Raef's experiences in the field, his ability to make complicated topics accessible to a non-practitioner audience, and his emphasis on laying out practical and understandable steps all serve to create a work that is as approachable as it is relevant.

I'm honored that he asked me to write this forward and I rest easy knowing that the readers of this book are in very capable hands. No topic could be more important.

Ed Moyle, Director of Thought Leadership and Research, ISACA

Introduction

In the brief time since you opened this book and started to read, more people, businesses and other organizations of all sizes have had their computers, accounts, mobile devices and other connected technologies compromised.

Most of these compromises are avoidable.

Without the right security precautions in place, connecting to the internet and using devices can feel like the digital wild west. Scams and ploys designed to compromise your personal and business devices are arriving with alarming and increasing frequency. Fall for just one and the cyber criminals can start to cause you substantial damage.

As we all put more information, trust and value in our online accounts and devices, we increase the value for cyber criminals to target them.

This book is designed to provide guidance on the basic security practices we can apply at home or in small businesses to help decrease the risk of being successfully attacked.

The guidance is kept simple, short and easy to follow, even if you have no technical knowledge. There is also a summary of the key points at the end of each chapter and a dictionary of any technical terms at the back of the book.

I have worked within the security field for over a decade now. During that time I have applied effective security to all kinds of environments, from home and small businesses, right through to writing the security and data privacy control framework for a few of the largest and most highly regulated organizations on the planet.

By applying the relatively simple security steps outlined in this book, it is possible to:

- Understand what actions and activities carry the most risk.
- Reduce the likelihood of being compromised by over 80%.
- Be more able to restore your devices if they have issues.

Read on and reduce your risk of your cybersecurity being compromised.

1: Understanding the Cyber Risk

It is barely possible to open any news web site without finding out about yet another leak of information or other cybersecurity breach by a large organization. MySpace, Mossack Fonseca, LinkedIn, Target, Sony, the NSA, the list goes on and on.

Yet large organizations tend to have significant amounts of money to invest to secure their systems and information.

When a person or small business gets successfully hit by a cyber attack, it very rarely becomes newsworthy.

Speak to only a few people and the likelihood is that they will have stories about how their own computer, laptop, online accounts or other devices were hit in some kind of online attack that cost them time, effort and money.

Cyber criminals require less and less technical expertise to design and perform successful attacks. That is leading to a large increase in the number of people engaging in these activities.

Cyber crime is very much like any other crime. The criminals are looking for the maximum return from minimum effort. As larger companies increase their security, an increasing number of cyber criminals are choosing to target private individuals and small companies because their generally lower levels of security make them easier to compromise.

There are various methods and techniques that can be used to perform a cyber attack. Most of the methods are surprisingly simple.

Often the attack involves getting the victim (or someone with access to an electronic device belonging to the victim) to simply click on a link, or open a document that in turn will install and initiate some form of malicious software (**malware**).

malware – *shortened version of* **malicious software**. *A disruptive, subversive or hostile program placed onto a* **digital device**. *These types of programs are usually disguised or embedded in a file that looks initially harmless but is actually designed to compromise a device or network of devices. There are many types of malware;* **adware, botnets, viruses, ransomware, scareware, spyware, trojans** *and* **worms**, *these are all examples of malware. Cyber criminals often use malware to mount* **cyber attacks**.

Cybersecurity: Home and Small Business

What undesirable activities any individual malicious software program might do can vary. It may be that the malicious software will lock you out of your own device and information, then demand a payment to release it. Malware can also be more insidious. It often sits quietly inside infected devices, secretly stealing information (including log-in and password details) for a long period of time.

Even large organizations can often find they have been compromised for months or even years before the unauthorized intrusion is detected.

Fortunately, it is relatively easy to significantly reduce the risk of this type of exposure by following some relatively easy security steps and processes. The aim of this book is to take you through those steps.

A good place to start is to define what we mean by the term 'cybersecurity'.

cybersecurity – *the protection of **digital devices** and their communication channels to keep them stable, dependable and reasonably safe from danger or threat. Usually the required protection level must be sufficient to prevent or address unauthorized access or intervention before it can lead to substantial personal, professional, organizational, financial and/ or political harm.*

digital device – *any electronic appliance that can create, modify, archive, retrieve or transmit information in an electronic format. Desktop computers, laptops, tablets, smart phones and internet connected home devices are all examples of **digital devices**.*

One of the main challenges in current cybersecurity is that the ***threat actors*** (the people interested in compromising your security) are constantly finding and sharing new ways to get into your devices and information.

Although having a good form of anti-malware software is an important factor in helping to reduce your risk, the reality is that this type of software will often (at best) only be able to help prevent 40% or less* of attacks.

* In 2014, even a Symantec executive, (Symantec being a leading supplier of antivirus software) admitted that their software at that time was probably only able to defeat around 45% of cyber attacks. *Source www.dottech.org.*

That does not make anti-malware software unimportant. It is still an effective way to reduce a substantial amount of risk.

For example, one bank revealed within the security community, that they had been scanning the devices customers were using to do their online banking for malware:

- What they discovered was that 50% of the customer devices contained known forms of malware.
- These are types of malware that could be eliminated if the customer had used good anti-malware on their device.
- They also found that informing customers that they had malware was harmful to the banks relationship with the customer, so they were not letting them know.

Installing effective anti-malware will reduce perhaps 40% of your risk. However, additional steps still need to be taken to help reduce your risk exposure further.

Often, when a new type of cyber threat emerges, it can be days, weeks or even years before an effective security countermeasure to eradicate the threat is created.

The speed that a countermeasure is created is usually related to how much solving the security problem is worth. If (for example), someone has created a very unique and complex form of attack that they have only used on a small number of low value targets, there may be insufficient financial motivation for the people that can create solutions to do so.

As an example, when the Sony organization was comprehensively hacked in 2014, although the software used was only a variation of a known form of malware, it still took the efforts of the best US government cybersecurity teams several weeks to crack the encryption and develop a solution. If the attack had not been so high profile, accessing those significant resources would not have been possible.

New forms of attack are referred to as a ***zero day attack***.

zero-day attack – *refers to the very first time a new type of exploit or new piece of malware is discovered. At that point in time, none of the anti-virus, anti-malware or other defenses may be set-up to defend against the new form of exploit.*

Part of the challenge is that there are literally hundreds of thousands of new types of malware being created every day. This is partly because malware can now be created very easily by people with little or no programming skill. They can use specialist software applications (such as Metasploit) that can put together new versions of malware as easily as most people can put together a Word document.

Some of the main security strategies we will cover in this book are steps to help reduce the risks of acquiring malware in the first place. Not acquiring malware in the first place is substantially cheaper than needing to remove it.

Before we start to enhance our own security, it is important to understand the cybersecurity risks better. We will now look at three key factors:

1. How does a cyber villain find and target a person or small business?

2. How a cyber attack on a person or small business is usually performed?

3. How frequently are these types of attacks taking place?

How Does a Person or Small Company Get Targeted?

There are two main routes to getting targeted:

- **You find the attacker.**
  You or someone with access to one of your electronic devices can accidentally find and click on a malicious link while surfing the internet, or open an online document that has malware within it or open a fake website. The malware that is then loaded into the device will identify you to the attackers.

  Another frequent method of attack is to encourage the user of a device to install something for 'free'. The free application can appear to be doing something very useful but it may also be running malicious and covert functions that can steal, lock or corrupt your information or devices.

- **The attacker finds you.**
  Depending on what you (or your company) do and how much you are worth, it may also be possible that you are more intentionally targeted for a cyber attack.

  With the amount of 'free' social media information and stolen lists of email addresses available, it is a low cost activity for attackers to send out millions of malicious links and documents to legitimate email addresses. They only need a small number of people to click on their link or open the document to make it worth their while.

There are many tools the cyber criminals can use (for example – one called 'Harvester') that can search through online sources (Facebook, LinkedIn and others) in order to find public information such as names, email address, phone numbers, job title and other address details for specific companies.

How Frequent are Cyber Attacks?

Cyber attacks are taking place all the time. There are literally millions of attempts to compromise accounts happening every second of every day. The reason that attacks are so common place is that many of the attacks are being run by automated tools.

Although many of those attacks are not focused on private individuals or small businesses, there are still a very large number that are. Most people receive attempts at cyber attacks every week. Some people who are very active online may receive attempts several times per day.

The good news is that most of those attempts at attack are currently passive, meaning that they require us (the recipient of the attack) to do something (click on a link or open an attachment) in order to be successful.

Usually if you do not click on (open) a malicious link, or open any attachment, the attack will be unsuccessful.

Always delete any message or communication you receive that contains any links or attachments from an unknown source. If you did not initiate the communication, the chances are very strong that any links or attachments will be an attempt to install malware.

How is a Cyber Attack Usually Performed?

In all cases, a cyber attacker is looking to find a weakness (a gap in your security) that it can exploit (take advantage of).

It is possible for a very sophisticated attacker to seek to force their way into your device. This is easier to do if you are running a device that has weak security configuration and is not using the very latest security patches from the operating system provider.

Always keep your digital devices up to date with the latest software patches from the manufacturer, especially for the operating system.

However, it is much easier (and more common) for a cyber attacker to get YOU the user of your device to unintentionally grant the attacker some type of access to your device by clicking on a malicious link or on a document they have loaded with malware.

Clicking on a Malicious Link or Document:

Getting anyone to click on a malicious link or open a document containing malware can be as simple as sending them an email, instant message or other online communication. This technique is known as **phishing**.

phishing – *using an electronic communication (for example email or instant messaging) that pretends to come from a legitimate source, in an attempt to get sensitive information (for example a password or credit card number) from the recipient. The methods of phishing have evolved so that the message can simply contain a link to an internet location where malware is situated or include an attachment (such as a PDF or Word document) that installs* **malware** *when opened. The malware can then be used to run any number of unauthorized functions, including stealing information from the device, replicating further malware to other accessible locations, sharing the user screen and logging keyboard entries.*

Often, these phishing attacks are sent to thousands or millions of recipients. However, there is also a more targeted version, known as **spear phishing**, where the communication is specifically sent to a more targeted set of users, for example, people who belong to a particular company or specific online service.

Using Insecure Connections:

If you use an insecure connection (such as a public Wi-Fi or unknown **Bluetooth** internet connection) it can be possible for your account details to be intercepted, or for a criminal to continue a session in an online account service, leaving you to think that your online session has finished and that you are logged out. This is called a **man-in-the-middle** attack and is covered in a later chapter.

Avoid using untrusted network connections (such as public Wi-Fi) and public locations to access any high value online accounts, such as payment systems and online banking.

Insecure connections also open up the possibility for an attacker to directly try to find any gaps in your device security. There are continual, automated software programs that are used to detect devices open to the internet and then look for known and open routes into them.

If your device has strong security, the latest software updates and does not use insecure connections, you will have put 3 defenses in place that make an intrusion of this type far less likely.

Getting a Phone Call from an Attacker (Vishing):

An increasingly popular form of attack is for a person to call you up with part of your information (perhaps only your name and phone number), pretending to be from a legitimate company, or from a law enforcement agency.

They will then ask you to perform an action. Whatever it is – don't do it!

Usually the action involves confirming your password information or can even be as simple as asking you to visit a particular website.

This technique is known as **vishing** (voice ph**ishing**) and is also covered in more detail in chapter 6.

If you receive an unsolicited call asking you to perform any kind of action or visit any kind of website. Do not be pushed into doing what they ask.

Vishing is a form of something known as **social engineering**.

Social Engineering:

*social engineering – The act of constructing relationships, friendships or other human interactions for the purpose of getting the recipient to perform an action or reveal information. The action or information revealed has the hidden purpose to achieve a nefarious objective, such as acquiring intelligence about the security, location or vulnerability of assets or even gaining the persons trust to open an internet link or document that will result in a **malware** foothold being created.*

One of the more substantial methods of social engineering, especially on individuals, is to befriend or become romantically involved with a target via an online platform. The attacker then uses this relationship to extort money by giving a seemingly compelling reason – they need money for a sick relative, or for an air fare to visit you.

This type of attack often yields the largest financial return as the attacker learns about you (from you) and just how much you may be able to afford to part with before they commit the act.

Theft amounts in the thousands and tens of thousands are not uncommon. Be very cautious of online 'friends' that you do not know from real life!

Stealing Your Information from Somewhere Else:

Thefts of large amounts of personal information from large and small organizations are unfortunately very common.

Reputable companies will usually own up to the loss of information and provide support to help their customers mitigate attempts to fraudulently use the information that has been stolen.

However, there is often a gap in time before the theft is discovered or announced.

If you ever access an account you own and notice any online account activity that is suspicious, you should immediately take 2 steps:

1) Report the activity to the service provider.
2) Immediately change your password for that account.

The Consequences of a Cyber Attack

The majority of cyber attacks on private individuals and small businesses that are successful are likely to result in one or more of the following consequences:

- Theft of information from the device.
- Theft of username and account details that you use through the compromised device. This in turn can be used to steal money or information from other online accounts, or set-up fake accounts that can incur you a personal loss.
- Ransom to release or restore information from your infected device or devices.
- Blackmail, if they discover any information that can be used to cause you personal damage (such as reputational loss).
- Spread of the infection to other devices that the infected device is permitted to connect to.
- Time, effort and financial cost to restore devices to a clean state.
- Loss of earnings and productivity if you have no secondary device that you can use in place of the one that is compromised.
- The covert use of your device to attack others.

This is not an exhaustive list; there are plenty of new ways to perform cyber attacks being devised all the time.

As we all start to buy and use more and more devices that are connected to the internet, we can expect new and more ingenious methods that cyber attackers will find to leverage them.

The important considerations to take away from this chapter are to understand that attempts at cyber attack are common place. They usually require YOU (the user) to have weak security, click on a link, visit a website, open a file or be overly trusting before the attack can be successful.

If you take the precautions outlined in this book, you will not completely eliminate your chances of being successfully attacked but you can reduce them by a substantial amount.

It is also important to note that once you get successfully attacked, the malware that is usually used will seek to remain in place, even if you attempt to reset or restore your device. This is known as **persistence.**

> **persistence** – *to seek continued existence in a situation despite opposition..*

One final security point worth making in this opening chapter is this:

> *If you do find (or suspect) that you have a digital device that has been compromised, never perform an insecure transfer of files between the device and an uninfected device. For example, if you copy files on to a USB stick, that is then likely to have the same infection and will spread it if inserted or connected to another device. Refer to the chapter on '****Recovering from a Cyber Attack****'.*

If you are interested in the most advanced method of cyber attack that is used, there is also a chapter near the end of the book specifically on the phenomena known as '***Advanced Persistent Threats***'

Chapter 1: Summary of Key Points:

- Cyber attacks on individuals and small businesses are increasing.
- Over 500,000 new forms of malicious software appear every day.
- Clicking on malicious content is the main method of attack.
- Using anti-malware software can still reduce risk by around 40%.

Always delete any message or communication you receive that contains any links or attachments from an unknown source. If you did not initiate the communication, the chances are very strong that any links or attachments will be an attempt to install malware.

Always keep your digital devices up to date with the latest software patches from the manufacturer, especially for the operating system.

Avoid using untrusted network connections (such as public Wi-Fi) and public locations to access any high value online accounts, such as payment systems and online banking.

If you receive an unsolicited call asking you to perform any kind of action or visit any kind of website. Do not be pushed into doing what they ask.

If you ever access an account you own and notice any online account activity that is suspicious, you should immediately take 2 steps:

1) Report the activity to the service provider.
2) Immediately change your password for that account.

If you do find (or suspect) that you have a digital device that has been compromised, never perform an insecure transfer of files between the device and an uninfected device. For example, if you copy files on to a USB stick, that USB stick is then likely to have the same infection and will spread it if inserted or connected to another device. Refer to the chapter on **'Recovering from a Cyber Attack'.**

2: **Identify** Where Your Risks Are

It does not matter if you are an individual or running a small business. You need to understand what assets of value you have to be able to protect them.

If you had a wallet stuffed with money, it would make sense that you would protect that more diligently than a packet of paper handkerchiefs.

The same principle applies to your electronic devices and the information you allow them to contain or access. It also applies to what information and risk you decide to take in any online accounts you choose to have.

If you put too much effort in to protecting low value assets, life gets unnecessarily hard. However, if you fail to adequately protect more valuable assets, then they will be exposed to higher levels of risk than they need to.

Cyber attackers are not interested in the digital equivalent of paper handkerchiefs, they are after the assets and information they can use to achieve the most financial (or political) gain.

For example, if I have a copy of a series of family photographs that I do not consider sensitive or embarrassing, I might consider these to be low risk. They are only a copy (so it does not matter if they are lost) and they contain nothing that can be misused or ransomed by any thief.

Conversely, I would be very concerned if my online bank account was accessed by a cyber criminal.

I take much higher security precautions on the password I use for sensitive online accounts. I only consider using secure devices (desktop, laptop, tablet or smart phone) on secure network connections to log-in to higher value accounts.

> *For high risk, high value devices and online accounts, always use a separate and complex password. It is also worthwhile using a discrete and different username if this is possible (some usernames are unfortunately locked to being your email address).*

Also be aware that one of the main forms of cyber attack involves criminals stealing usernames and passwords (often in bulk) from one online service, then trying that same username and password combination in higher value accounts such as payment services.

> *Never re-use the same username and password combination on any accounts of value.*

It can be hard to stay on top of all those different usernames and passwords. Some people choose to write those details down somewhere in full. This is a risky practice. If someone gets access to that information, your account can be compromised. However, there is a solution I have created.

> *You can store a physical log of your username and passwords using* **'The Encrypted Book of Passwords'** *as this allows you to keep part of the information secret, so anyone accessing your book would still not be able to access the accounts, unless you reveal your secret keys.*

Four Steps to Cybersecurity

For the purposes of this book, we are going to use a simple, 4 step cybersecurity model:

- **Identify**   (your valuable assets)
- **Protect**   (with appropriate security)
- **Detect**   (any compromised account or device)
- **Recover**   (replace or restore any compromised asset)

In this chapter, we will focus on helping to identify what electronic assets and information you have that is of value.

You will notice that some other chapters that introduce the other steps (protect, detect and recover) have that name at the front of the chapter title.

If you were a large company seeking to insure your organization against the potential losses from a cyber attack, the insurer would be likely to only insure the risks that meet the following criteria:

- **You have to identify the specific sets of information you want to insure.**
- For each set of information, you have to check that there is adequate security in place, appropriate to the information value.
- If you find there are any major or critical gaps in the security, you must address those gaps before the information can be insured.

The very first step is to identify what information you would like to safeguard. You may initially think that what you would like to safeguard is *everything*. However, applying really strong security to everything can be expensive and impractical.

It is worth thinking through and identifying what the highest value electronic information you have is.

Most home and small business users start by thinking they would treat the security on all of their devices the same. However, once you identify what information and online accounts of value you have, a more practical approach is often to apply different levels of security to different devices, depending on what they will be accessing or storing.

As an example, I have some very low value android tablets that I use for general surfing of the internet. They include a separate email account. I consider these devices to be compromised (to contain malware) even if they do not. I re-build them (factory reset) regularly. I tend to think of these as my 'junk' devices.

If I receive a potential ***phishing*** email on a secure device that I would like to check, in case it is genuine, I can choose to send it to a junk device to open and inspect via the separate email address.

This approach may sound expensive, however, a basic (cheap) tablet can cost from around $50, far cheaper than having my valuable information stolen. It is also cheaper than the cost I would incur to reset and restore my more secure device.

If you do want to access potentially harmful websites, or open potentially harmful attachments or links, do it on a device that you don't mind messing up! This is usually a cheap device that you can easily perform a factory reset on. Make sure you own the device, do not mess up other peoples devices. Also be aware that factory resets do not always get rid of malware.

Identifying Your Riskiest Information & Accounts

When you first start improving your cybersecurity, even as a home user, you might think that applying high security to everything is the way to go.

More specifically if we try and apply high security to every digital device we own and operate (laptop, desktop, tablet, smart phone, smart thermostat, ...) then we can often find ourselves with equally bad security everywhere.

However, if you stop to consider what information and online accounts we have that are of highest value, it is then possible to take a more robust approach to keeping those assets secure.

Major organizations that have effective security follow the same kind of approach. They have separate zones with different levels of security, so that they can keep their highest value information more secure than their day-to-day, lower value, lower risk information.

What we will do in this section is to help you think through the information and online accounts you have that present the most significant personal risk to you or business risk to your small company.

The first thing to do is to draw up a list of what you consider to be the information and accounts of value. You can (if you like) use a sticky note pad to write each one down. For example:

- Online banking details
- Sensitive personal documents
- PayPal account
- Ebay account
- Facebook account
- Photo archive
- Primary email account
- Dating website log-in details
- Linked-In login details
- Old (electronic) documents
- ...

As you can see from the example above, this is usually a mixture of online accounts and (potentially) electronic files. Your electronic files may be locally stored (on a hard disk or USB key), stored with an online provider, or in multiple locations.

Once you have your list, you are then going to start to sort them into 3 piles, to reflect their value and sensitivity if they were to become stolen, damaged, or completely unavailable for a time. Let's call the piles:

- **Very high risk** (devastating if compromised)
- **Medium risk** (damaging but recoverable if compromised)
- **Low risk** (inconvenient but not damaging if compromised).

It can sometimes help to assign a theoretical financial value to each category above.

To help you further, this is the basic way any organization typically thinks through the risk level against each information asset and online account:

- **Confidentiality**
  What level of financial or reputational damage would I (or my organization) suffer if this information or asset was accessed or a copy of the contents were stolen or used by an attacker?

- **Integrity**
  What level of financial or reputational damage would I (or my organization) suffer if the information in this asset was changed or corrupted by an attacker? For example, in an account that is used to update a website or Twitter feed, what would happen if an attacker could add or change the content?

- **Availability**
  What level of financial or reputational damage would I (or my organization) suffer if this content was completely inaccessible for a time? The shorter the amount of time you could be without the content, the higher the risk. As an example, if you run a small accountancy firm, then the accounts themselves may be critical to be able to access in order to do business.

Items with high risk to confidentiality or integrity demand higher levels of security.

Items that need high availability need to be backed up regularly and have a contingency solution in place. This is so you can get those items back up and running quickly if they are attacked.

Items with high risk to availability will require that you make frequent backups (copies) of the information into a separate location. The backup location should be somewhere secure and separate from the master information. That means taking a copy to somewhere that will

> *not be compromised if your main devices and data are. This could be an encrypted USB key, or a secure cloud storage service. If you have a small business or home network, it is not advisable to keep backup copies of information only on your local network. If you do (and your network is compromised) you may otherwise still lose your backup information.*

By understanding what your highest risk information and online account assets are, you will be able to make more informed choices about where you will access them from and the minimum level of security you will apply to each of them.

Identifying Your Digital Devices

A few years ago, a US police department was caught out after it disposed of its old photocopiers. It turned out that the photocopiers contained a storage device capable of retaining thousands of images. As a standard feature, the photocopier was storing a copy of each document that it copied.

Criminal records, scene of crime reports and more were found to be present.

The lesson to be learned from this is that when we think about the list of electronic devices that we need to apply security to, we may need to think further than just our laptops, tablets and smart phones.

With the increase in the ***internet of things***, more of us are choosing to add new, connected devices to both the home and small business environment.

__Internet of Things (IoT)__ – the incorporation of electronics into everyday items sufficient to allow them to network (communicate) with other network capable devices. For example, to include electronics in a home thermostat so that it can be operated and share information over a network connection to a smart phone or other network capable devices.

In the case of the photocopier, it was not even the ability to network that created the compromise. It was just the unsafe disposal of the item.

> *When you are ready to retire or re-sell any electronic device, be very sure to fully remove and destroy any sensitive information it contains. A factory reset, or pressing 'delete' does not usually destroy the information. Specialist software is usually required.*

A good suggestion is to only re-sell devices that are reset and have never contained sensitive information. In the case of a smart phone, wipe the device first using specialist software, perform a manufacturer reset and change the passwords of any accounts that it stored before selling it on. That will not completely remove the risk but it will substantially reduce it.

If the device you want to dispose of has had high value information on it, you will need to delete that information and then run specialist deletion software that is built to make deleted information unrecoverable.

Now that you are thinking more about your current electronic devices, you can again grab some sticky notes and list any device you consider holds or accesses information or online accounts of value on to separate notes.

- Desktop computers
- Laptops
- Tablets
- Smart phones
- Smart watches
- Other smart devices that have storage capability.

This time we are going to do 2 things.

Firstly, we will think about what each device currently accesses from our information and online account list. Based on the highest risk type they are currently accessing, place the device in one of 3 piles:

- **Very high risk** (devastating if compromised)
- **Medium risk** (damaging but recoverable if compromised)
- **Low risk** (inconvenient but not damaging if compromised).

The second activity is to consider if each of the devices on the high and medium risk piles needs to access the high or medium risk information or accounts. It is okay if they do, however, any devices that you can use to store or access only low risk assets will be able to be used more flexibility (with lower security) than those that access high or medium risk information.

Any devices where you can conveniently and safely remove access to high and medium risk information can be flagged with an asterisk (*) and moved to your low risk pile.

You will need to remove the medium and high risk information from those devices.

Planning Security Based on Risk

Now that we know what our high, medium and low risk information assets, online accounts and electronic devices are, we can make more informed choices about where to increase our security. This will in turn help to reduce the risk of being vulnerable to cyber attack.

This is a very similar process to ones used by large organizations.

- We have classified our information based on the risks it can present to us.
- We have then classified our digital devices (laptops, computers, tablets, smart phones) based on what information they will be accessing.

This will be very useful later on when we look to increase our cybersecurity. We can now choose to apply the greatest level of security on the information and devices that present the greatest risk to us.

The reason we might choose to apply higher security only on selected devices is that it takes time, effort and additional cost to do it. High security devices are also less flexible in what we allow them to do.

Chapter 2: Summary of Key Points:

- The four main steps to cybersecurity are:
  - **Identify** (your valuable assets)
  - **Protect** (with appropriate security)
  - **Detect** (any compromised account or device)
  - **Recover** (replace or restore any compromised asset)
- Start by identifying assets that present the highest risk to you.
  - Sets of high-value electronic files
  - Valuable online accounts
  - Items that damage you if stolen or unavailable.
- Only perform high value tasks on secure devices over secure connections.

For high risk, high value devices and online accounts, always use a separate and complex password. It is also worthwhile using a discrete and different username if this is possible (some usernames are unfortunately locked to being your email address).

Never re-use the same username and password combination on any accounts of value.

You can store a physical log of your username and passwords using **'The Encrypted Book of Passwords'** *as this allows you to keep part of the information secret, so anyone accessing your book would still not be able to access the accounts, unless you reveal your secret keys.*

If you do want to access potentially harmful websites, or open potentially harmful attachments or links, do it on a device that you don't mind messing up!

Backups (copies) of important information should be stored in a secure location away from your main network and devices.

When you are ready to retire or re-sell any electronic device, be very sure to fully remove and destroy any sensitive information it contains. A factory reset, or pressing 'delete' does not usually destroy the information. Specialist software is usually required.

3: Who are the Cyber Villains? (Threat Actors)

In this section we will briefly review the different types of people and organizations that perform cyber attacks and other unwanted intrusions, or who simply might misuse access to them causing some kind of disruption or unwanted disclosure of information.

There are eight potential threat groups, the first two (organized criminal groups and insiders) are the most likely to represent the largest threat to the typical home and small business scenarios.

As we look through some of the other six categories, it is worth considering that although our own home or small business based technologies may not be under any direct threat from them, we often rely on and use other critical services (such as banking, power, water, transport and major online storage services) that are.

If we want to take a holistic view of our cybersecurity, we need to also consider, where possible, what organizations to trust.

The eight main categories of entities that may perform cyber intrusions are:

1. **Organized criminal groups.**
   Cyber attacks are now big business and are mostly run just like commercial enterprises, involving a team of people with different skills engaging in different parts of the attack process.

2. **Insiders** (people with access to one or more of your devices)
   Whether intentional or just through unintentional misuse, a substantial amount of the disruption or unwanted disclosure of information happens through people that have legitimate access to our devices.

3. **Legitimate companies** engaging in profit optimization
   Many legitimate organizations aim to embed permissions and software functions inside other items you want in order to collect information about you, promote their products and services and even look to use some of your devices power and bandwidth to provide their services.

4. **Terrorist groups**
   Terrorist group primary goals are always centered on damage to their adversary and that is seldom a home or small business. However,

many also choose to raise funds by operating some of their cyber capabilities on committing cyber crime.

5. **Professional Hackers**

   Most skilled, professional *hackers* in developed countries can earn better money by working ethically for companies and organizations, identifying their security vulnerabilities. As a private individual or small business, you are unlikely to get targeted by any independent professional hacker, unless they are specifically sponsored by an adversary.

6. **Amateur Hackers** (and journalists)

   As committing cyber crime requires less and less skill, there are a small number of people who may try and 'have a go' at random or even local targets. There are also frequent instances of journalists (aspiring and amateur) trying to use cyber techniques to obtain information. These are usually clumsy efforts that will not beat secure environments, often leave a trail back to the perpetrator and are not currently happening that often. Amateur hacking is more likely to happen in places of high population density (hacking into and using internet bandwidth) and places where the subject of cyber attacks and defenses may be studied (Universities). Amateur attacks are currently less likely to create damage even if they are successful.

7. **Hacktivist Communities**

   Hacktivism is the act of breaking into devices or systems to further a political or socially motivated objective. Hacktivists only target people and businesses if they are known to be connected to a political or social activity that is considered unethical by their group.

8. **Nation States**

   Most nation states engage in quite a range of cyber attack and defense activities designed to optimize their power and strengthen their protection. Generally only high profile people, or those with privileged access to critical national infrastructure, high value intellectual property or large scale digital services are targeted. However, some nation state employees are not averse to 'recycling' anything their government is not interested in for their own financial gain.

Part of what motivates and drives what categories of potential attackers may target you or your small business organization will depend on:

- What you do (personally and professionally),
- How wealthy you are,
- If you have been successfully compromised before,
- And where you are physically located or travelling with your devices.

'What you do' includes factors such as; (i) If you engage in a lot of riskier online behaviors (surfing to dubious and unknown websites, using your devices on insecure, public networks). (ii) Whether you are someone (or an organization) that has a high profile, or engages in political or other activities that can be the subject for political or ethical attacks. (iii) What kind of information you store or transact through your devices (for example, lots of financial transactions, lots of sensitive records such as medical information or high value intellectual property, …) and (iv) What organizations you are connected to or do business with (for example - can your access be used as a potential route of entry into another person or organizations systems or devices).

By identifying who is most likely to target you, you can (later on) focus on strengthening your security approach appropriate to those threats.

As organized cyber crime and insider threats account for most of the cyber attack risks that can face individuals, let's take a closer look at those two areas:

Organized Criminal Groups

Although there are independent cyber criminals, the range of skills used means that cyber crime is much more lucrative when they are run like proper businesses.

Organized criminal cyber groups often have one set of people who collect information on targets, another group who put together the attack tools (fraudulent websites, infected documents, other forms of malware, …), different people who sell information and even call center operators with banks of desks to call out to potential victims.

They achieve their financial goals by a number of methods including:

- Holding the recovery of your own information to ransom (see **ransomware** in the next chapter)

- Stealing account and password information from you (or a service provider) and making unauthorized use of those details, for example making fraudulent transactions from your accounts.
- Stealing a copy of valuable information from you and selling it on to others.
- Stealing information of value about you from other organizations where they have been able to compromise their security. For example, stealing username and password details in bulk from an insecurely built or configured online service.
- Using the access you or your device has into another organization or device and then stealing or ransoming that other party.

The structure, scale and organization of these groups mean they can mount strong attacks and make faster, better use of what they steal before counter security or law enforcement can catch up.

They also usually operate from geographic territories that are far away from their victims. That helps them to stay out of reach from any easy prosecution or repercussions.

Their main methods of initial attack (especially due to the geographic distance) usually involve getting the victim to install malware (by clicking a link or opening an attachment) or getting a person to disclose information (for example through a fake website or via a phone call) that can then be used to access one or more of your online accounts, or even disable your smart phone, laptop or other devices.

Insiders

Many 'home user' insider threats are entirely accidental or unintentional. A person with legitimate (authorized) access to one or more of your devices may accidentally do something that results in compromising your security.

This can be as simple as clicking on a malicious link from an email, search engine or even a text message.

This is usually because they have not had enough cybersecurity education and training.

However, it is also worth remembering that many cyber attacks, especially in small businesses can be due to disaffected or opportunist insiders. These are people who may be tempted or motivated to intentionally steal, disclose or corrupt your information.

Take care about who you permit to access your devices or online accounts, especially where they contain sensitive information. Do they really need the access? If they do, what protective controls can you put in place to prevent accidental or intentional misuse? (You will find options in later chapters that cover security steps that can be used to help guard against these threats).

> *The possibility of insiders creating either intentional or accidental exposure of your information can be reduced by restricting their access to the minimum they need. For example, not providing any unnecessary permissions to the user (for example - no **administrative access**) or to not allow them to access certain equipment or information.*

The main insider that can create the most unintentional damage is likely to be YOU.

> *Even though you may need privileged access to install new software to your device, many devices allow you to separate or password protect that function. If you do all of your day-to-day activities in a low privilege account (no administrative access) you can always switch into a higher privilege account only when you intentionally want to add software or re-configure security settings.*

We can all get complacent (it has happened to me) and use the wrong account or device to access something that initially looks harmless.

The devices you own and manage are reliant on you using them securely, take care about what you surf to or install. It only takes a single click to infect your device. An infected device can then quickly go on to spread that infection to everything they have a trusted connection to.

Legitimate Companies

Any good commercial organization has to focus on generating profit. Profit optimization relies on maximizing revenues and minimizing costs. That relies on having the best possible information about your customers and encouraging them to buy your products and services.

It is important to be clear that I am not suggesting that any truly legitimate company will set out to intentionally attack any of your accounts or digital devices.

What most of them will do is try to embed permissions and software functions inside other items you want in order to collect information about you, promote their products and services and even look to use some of your devices power and bandwidth to provide their services.

We have all experienced **nagware**.

nagware – *a form of software that persistently reminds the user that they should do something even though they might not want to. This is not usually considered malicious software but it does exhibit some unwanted features, disrupting the flow of the users' interaction with their device. Nagware is often used as partial payment for some forms of software, especially free software.*

It is unfortunately very usual for legitimate companies to bundle all kinds of software functions that spy (**spyware**), nag (**nagware**) or place targeted advertising (**adware**) on our machines.

Although you do not necessarily need to do anything about these, you can often find very informative guidance on how to remove and disable many of these functions. For example, one of the most used desktop and laptop operating systems includes many default settings that allow them to use your computer to send out updates to other computers, monitor your preferences and provide you with preferred advertising content. Almost all of these features can be removed or opted out from if you are willing to spend a few hours of effort and research on YouTube!

Any free software, even from a trusted source is even more likely to include components that require permission to monitor your online behavior and send you targeted advertising.

Wherever practical, always keep the number of installed software applications to a minimum. That will help to keep your devices running faster and decrease the amount of **nagware**, **spyware** *and* **adware** *you are exposed to. Uninstall software that you no longer need or use.*

It is likely that these functions will be the subject of further legislation in future. Many legitimate companies seek to navigate the edge of what current privacy regulations permit. They cannot afford to have less customer intelligence than their competition if they want to survive.

I have included 'legitimate companies' as a potential threat actor here because they can create unexpected intrusions into privacy, disruption to your user experience and even create unexpected cost by using your devices power and bandwidth.

Those legitimate companies are also (themselves) frequently targeted for cyber attacks. Be careful what legitimate companies you choose to trust. You can be susceptible to an indirect attack, for example, if your bank or online payment provider has a system that gets compromised, will they be losing your money or theirs?

Chapter 3: Summary of Key Points:

- The main direct threats to home & small business usually come from:
  - Organized criminal groups
  - Insiders (intentional and unintentional compromise)
- What threat actors may target you depends on:
  - What you do.
  - What you have (financially and information value).
  - Your location: Where you are and where you go.
  - If you have been compromised before.
- Organized criminal groups are usually the biggest threat.
- Consider what other threat actors may target you.

*The possibility of insiders creating either intentional or accidental exposure of your information can be reduced by restricting their access to the minimum they need. For example, not providing any unnecessary permissions to the user (for example - no **administrative access**) or to not allow them to access certain equipment or information.*

*Wherever practical, always keep the number of installed software applications to a minimum. That will help to keep your devices running faster and decrease the amount of **nagware**, **spyware** and **adware** you are exposed to. Uninstall software that you no longer need or use.*

Even though you may need privileged access to install new software to your device, many devices allow you to separate or password protect that function. If you do all of your day-to-day activities in a low privilege account (no administrative access) you can always switch into a higher privilege account only when you intentionally want to add software or re-configure security settings.

4: Security Preparation and Planning

Before we move into covering the steps to secure your devices and accounts, it is exceptionally helpful to have a basic plan in mind.

Most of us have more than one device; perhaps a laptop, smart phone and a tablet device.

We could choose to apply very high security to everything. However, if all our devices have high value content, we effectively have no way to safely engage in any higher risk online activity. For example, we cannot randomly click on search engine links from high value devices for fear that the site may contain malware. (Although there are security programs that can block 'known' malicious links, there are always some that can escape the process.)

It also takes more time and effort to set-up and maintain high security on devices.

Back in chapter 2, you will have worked out what information and devices you have and how you would classify the value and impact if they were compromised.

Although we are encouraged to trust and share information openly across all of our devices, this is in fact a very poor security practice. My smart phone is already a valuable enough item to steal. Sure, I can also turn it into a credit card style payment system and add every sensitive document I have to it, then take it out when I go for a social drink. The question is – do I want to?

Every person and their risk appetite are different. Every small business and their risk appetite are also different.

You can take any decision you want to about what content and security you choose to put on each of your devices.

You often also have options to enhance the security on many of your online accounts.

Your security strategy and plan is your own choice. I do, however, recommend that you plan your security.

What I mean by planning your security is that you decide what devices to apply high security to based on the balance between your needs and the security risks.

It may be that you have to put a lot of very high value content on to your smart phone. In that case, apply the high security measures for mobile devices that are outlined in this book. This includes a ***mobile device management*** solution that can remotely wipe your device and even identify where it is located, should it (for example) be stolen.

Conversely, you might want to have at least one device, both at home, at work and travelling around, that accesses and contains practically nothing of value. Although it is still a good idea to apply basic security measures (anti-malware software including a device firewall), you then have a safer place to check out any potentially risky links or attachments.

> *Never give devices that have low security any trusted connection access to any of your high security devices. For example, if I have a low security tablet, I should not be connecting it to the internet through a smart phone that I have chosen to apply high security to.*

> *Whenever you are storing or transacting high value, high risk information, you should only do that from high security devices over known, high security trusted networks.*

It is worth emphasizing that good security does cost time and money to apply.

Remember also that even the best security can be compromised. This is because new threats (***zero day attacks***) are constantly emerging and there is always a lag between the threats being identified and the protection being available.

> ***zero-day*** *– refers to the very first time a new type of **exploit** or new piece of **malware** is discovered. At that point in time, none of the anti-virus, anti-malware or other defenses may be set-up to defend against the new form of exploit.*

Just because you apply high security does not mean you will be digitally bulletproof. It will, however, decrease your potential to be compromised.

A basic plan can be as simple as just thinking through what devices you currently have and deciding which ones will be:

- **High security** – for the devices you will use to access and store or transact your most valuable information and online account activities.
- **Medium security** – for the devices that may deal with some information of value.

- **Standard security** – for any low value device that you expect not to transact any valuable information on.

As we move through how to protect devices and online accounts, we will identify if each security measure is recommended as a high, medium or standard security approach.

Standard security indicates a control that should be applied, whenever possible, to **all devices**, no matter what you use them for.

Medium security indicates a control that should be applied to **all medium and high security devices or accounts**, wherever possible. That means to devices that you will use to access, transact or store medium or high risk access to information or services.

High security should be applied to any high security device. That means apply this control to devices and accounts, whenever possible, if they access, transact or store any information that if compromised, could result in significant financial, personal or professional damage.

Keep in mind that you can change the way you use a device to reflect the level of security you choose to apply.

Remember also that if you delete data from a device through a normal delete function, it is usually still present (the device operating system simply flags the file so that it can be overwritten in future.

Only deleting information using specialist deletion software will truly remove information from a device to the extent that it will be unlikely to be recovered. This type of deletion software usually overwrites the file multiple times with new information to help obscure the electronic data that it replaced.

That means that if you decide to change a devices usage down to a lower security level, take care to make absolutely sure any higher security level information or access is sufficiently removed.

Chapter 4: Summary of Key Points:

- Identify what devices you consider to require high, medium or standard security.
- Apply standard security to all devices and accounts.
- Apply medium security to all high and medium security devices and accounts.
- Apply high security to all high security devices and accounts.

Never give devices that have low security any trusted connection access to any of your high security devices. For example, if I have a low security tablet, I should not be connecting it to the internet through a smart phone that I have chosen to apply high security to.

Whenever you are storing or transacting high value, high risk information, you should only do that from high security devices over known, high security trusted networks.

Only deleting information using specialist deletion software will truly remove information from a device to the extent that it will be unlikely to be recovered. This type of deletion software usually overwrites the file multiple times with new information to help obscure the electronic data that it replaced.

5: **Protect:** Basic Methods of Cyber Defense

If you have followed the steps in this book, you should now have identified:

- Your information of highest risk and value.
- What digital devices and accounts you will apply high, medium or standard security to.
- What kinds of attacks and attackers are most likely to occur?

Remember to apply standard security to all devices as a minimum, wherever possible.

Due to the wide variety of device types and operating systems available, these steps describe the security objectives to achieve. They do not recommend the specific software to use, or how to install on any particular platform.

To make this section as easy to use as possible, the security steps are laid out by the types of devices or accounts they should be applied to:

- Devices with operating systems
- Additional options for mobile devices
- USB storage and local network storage devices
- Online accounts and password management
- Network access points (Wi-Fi and similar)
- Email & messaging
- Locally connected hardware (printers, etc)
- Internet of Things devices
- Disposal of devices and electronic information

Devices with Operating Systems

The security measures described in this section should be applied to all devices where the operating system or platform permits.

That includes tablets (iPads, Android), smart phones, laptops, desktop computers, even to more sophisticated smart watches and other internet connectible devices.

Mobile devices should also look to apply the additional measures described in the section dedicated to them.

Remember that *definitions for any items in bold and italics* can be found at the back of the book.

Security Control	Security Level

o Install a good security software solution on each device.
   o That means install security software on every desktop, laptop, tablet, smart phone or other smart device that you own.
   o A good security solution will include the functions of *anti-malware*, a device *firewall* and *intrusion prevention*.
   o For high security mobile devices, check what security may be bundled in with any *mobile device management* solution you choose to install (see the section on mobile) and add any functions that are missing as additional security software.
	Standard

o Always keep your software, especially your operating system, up to date with the latest software updates.
   o This is one of the most important and basic steps for robust security. As security vulnerabilities are discovered, good manufacturers release updates to rectify them.
   o Most forms of malware are designed to compromise only devices that still have open vulnerabilities (have not had the latest software updates (patches) applied).
	Standard

o Ensure anyone who uses or accesses your digital devices are educated against opening links or documents from unknown sources, installing untrusted software, or surfing to unknown sites. These are some of the main methods cyber criminals use to infiltrate devices. o Chapter 6 of this book has been designed to help. If you have other users who access your securely configured device – get them to read that chapter.	Standard

Security Control	Security Level
o Remove any unnecessary or unused software. o If you know you are definitely not using a particular piece of software, remove it. This will reduce potential monitoring and backdoor vulnerabilities on your device.	Standard

o Only install new software from trusted sources.
    o Remember that software from untrusted sources is more likely to have the potential to include ***malware***.
    o Free software usually includes some form of payment by requiring certain access to information on your device, or by including ***nagware, adware, spyware*** and other functions that can share information about you, your online behavior and your device contents.
	Standard

o Manage the device access accounts so that each person is using only the minimum level of access privilege that is required.
    o In real terms, this usually means that if your device has the ability to restrict the right to install software (often known as '***administrative permissions***') to selected accounts, only permit that elevated permission on the accounts where it is required.
    o Any administrative account should only be used when you are installing or uninstalling software. If someone needs that level of access, it is a good idea to give them 2 accounts, one for everyday use (no administrative permissions) and one for when they need to make configuration or software changes to the device.
    o If you are usually operating a device without the permission to install software or make configuration changes, it substantially reduces the possibility of accidentally installing malware, or for attacks to open up holes in your security configuration.
	Standard

Security Control	Security Level
○ Regularly ***backup*** (store a copy) of the information you have that is of value to you. This must be stored away from the device itself. That means there should be no connection (electronic or otherwise) between the device and your backup location except for during the backup process. 　○ What you choose to backup and how frequently should depend on the value of that information to you. 　○ The purpose of backup is to help restore your valuable information in the event that your device(s) are infected or stolen. This is covered in the chapter on 'Recovering from a Cyber Attack'. 　○ Some cloud backup solutions have the ability to safely capture a separate, remote and encrypted copy each time the process is run. That will provide more recovery options if you discover some backups are themselves corrupted. 　○ Never keep your backup device on a trusted connection to the information it is safeguarding. If you do and your main information is infected, you are likely to find your backup information has also been compromised. For example - if you use USB keys to perform a local backup, keep in mind that attaching it to an infected device can compromise the existing backup information it already holds.	Standard
○ Never click on any unexpected or uninvited banners that appear. 　○ If you have pop-ups appearing on screen, even when your browser is off, this can be an ***indicator of compromise*** (IoC). That means your machine is potentially already infected – but the infection may be treatable. Refer to the chapter on 'Recovering from a Cyber Attack' if this applies to you.	Standard

Security Control	Security Level

o Only set-up networks and trusted connections between devices where you absolutely need to. Trusted connections include **Bluetooth**, **NFC** (near field communications) and any other route that shares electronic data streams between devices.
  o Setting up trusted connections provides the ability for any cyber attack to spread between devices just like a cold can spread between people that meet.
  o By keeping devices as separate as possible, you prevent most forms of cyber attack from being able to spread and cause greater damage.
	Standard

o Always lock your computer screen back to requiring a username and password. On most Microsoft Windows operating systems, this can be achieved by clicking CTRL + ALT + DEL keys and then selecting the option to LOCK SCREEN. o You would be surprised how often leaving a computer unlocked results in an unexpected intrusion.	Standard

o Turn on your **device encryption**, or install it if it is not part of the operating system.
  o This will help reduce the risk of your information becoming accessible if the device is lost or stolen. If the thief cannot break into a legitimate device account or break the encryption, the information will not be readable by them.
  o Note that this only secures the information at rest on the device when there is no legitimate user logged on. Other security steps are required to secure or encrypt information whenever it is sent or received.
	Medium

o Install a security solution to filter and block access to any known malicious **URLs** (links and websites).
  o This may be bundled in with your main security software.
  o This will reduce (but not eliminate) the risk of opening links to malware and fraudulent websites.
	Medium

Security Control	Security Level

o Only connect your device to the internet using a secure and trusted connection.
  o Jumping on to an unknown 'free' internet connection, especially when travelling in densely populated areas can lead to attacks such as **man-in-the-middle**.
  o If you do use these connections, be aware that you will be at risk from fake connections and that interceptions of data can take place.
  o It is inadvisable to use unknown connections for high value transactions, such as internet banking.
	Medium

o Check and adjust any privacy settings on the operating system. Manufacturers often bundle in many options in their initial software agreement that include some pretty intrusive privacy options by default.
  o There are also usually ways to adjust those settings and remove permissions. (Opting out of privacy intrusions is a legal requirement in most territories). However, you will usually have to do some research on where those options have been hidden.
  o A sign of a really intrusive company is when they make opting out of their privacy intrusions into a sport that takes hours to complete.
  o You do not have to remove these options, however – they do protect your privacy and usage information. If you do not, you can find that you are likely to be sent targeted advertising straight to your screen, have some information (including contacts) disclosed and even some of your bandwidth and processor power used.
  o Because this step can take a lot of time and the intrusion it combats is usually irritating rather than damaging – consider this optional but advisable.
	Medium

Security Control	Security Level

o   If you have a critical reliance on the device, you will need a viable action plan to restore and use an equivalent device in the event the device is lost, stolen or compromised.
   o   As an example – I hold an encrypted log of my accounts and passwords (in ***The Encrypted Book of Passwords***) and also an encrypted backup copy of the critical files away from the main device.
   o   In the event my high security device is stolen, I can enable a spare or literally buy a replacement and have it up and running, with my files and contacts in less than an hour.
   o   See also the section on mobile devices for the capability to remotely wipe missing or stolen devices.
	High

Additional Options for Mobile Devices

Remember, these steps for mobile devices that should be applied <u>in addition</u> to all of those described under '**Devices with Operating Systems**'

Security Control	Security Level
o Use a strong form of screen lock, such as a long PIN (6 or more characters) or password protection. o BEWARE: Unlock patterns on touch screen devices often leave grease marks on screens allowing the pattern to be easily guessed. Short PINs with repeating numbers can also be open to this vulnerability.	Standard
o Make sure that the screen is set to lock within a relatively short amount of inactivity (for example 1 minute). o In the event that your device is taken, it makes it less likely that it will already be 'unlocked'.	Standard

Security Control	Security Level
o Remember to consider the physical security of your mobile devices. They are more open to potential theft. Keep them as secure as possible. Most thefts that happen are opportunist because a device is left unsupervised on a table or desk.	Standard
o Switch off Bluetooth, wireless and other connection types when they are not in active use. o Open Bluetooth and other connections can be used to infiltrate your device.	Medium
o The best security software (especially for mobile devices) can include the ability to locate the device and even remotely lock or delete the contents. This is known as a **mobile device management** solution. It may be separately installed or bundled with the other security features (anti-malware, firewall and intrusion prevention). o Remember to keep your mobile device management access details secure. If they are compromised, they can be used as a point of attack to lock out or wipe your device.	High

USB Storage & Local Network Storage Devices

Keep offline when possible

Security Control	Security Level
o Be careful of re-using backup media (such as USB storage) across different devices unless you have a high confidence that they are all clear of malware. Sharing USB and other storage devices has the same potential to spread digital infections as people sharing needles have on biological infections.	Standard

Security Control	Security Level
o When your storage device is not in use, keep it switched off or disconnected. o Remarkably, many of the breaches that result in the loss of information take place because information that really did not need to be left online, was left online.	Medium

o Think about what you choose to store to any device, how long you keep it for and whether it needs to be online (instantly available) or can be physically archived (for example on a securely stored and encrypted USB storage device).
    o Many of the very public breaches of cyber security have resulted in revealing information that was old and not required to be held 'online'. As an example, if some of these breached companies had archived their email every year or two, the damage would have been a fraction of what it was.
    o Keep rarely used information offline and destroy it totally when it is no longer required.
	High

Online Accounts & Password Management

Security Control	Security Level
o Select your online service providers with the care appropriate to the value of the information or service they will be providing to you: o If an online account provider hits the press frequently with major breaches, it is worth changing away from that provider. It can take years for a provider to fix security effectively – because the root cause is often cultural and not just a one-off technical issue.	Standard

Cybersecurity: Home and Small Business

Security Control	Security Level
o Use a separate and complex password for each account you use to access a device or online account. o You must also keep that information secret and never disclose it to anyone. You can use solutions like '*The Encrypted Book of Passwords*' to store that information securely without the possibility of it being exposed from that format by any cyber attack.	Standard
o Never write down your username and password details in a format that can be viewed or stolen. Never share your passwords with anyone. o With the sheer number of accounts, it can be tempting to write passwords down. Don't do it.	Standard
o If you find that an account and password has been compromised, or if you inadvertently disclose the information, change the password immediately.	Standard
o Take care not to use easy passwords or easily guessable patterns to set your passwords. o For example – if you use a password combination like part of the website URL and a consistent secret key – then the loss of one password can allow attackers to open any of your accounts.	Standard
o Do not choose options that allow you to remain logged in to online accounts. o If you select the option to remain logged in, any unauthorized access to your device will also allow access to your online accounts.	Standard

o Apply appropriate configuration to any privacy settings.
    o Social media and other accounts often have privacy settings that can determine who your information can be accessible to.
    o Applying appropriate secrecy and privacy options can help to hide your email address and other information from potential cyber attackers.
	Standard

Security Control	Security Level
o Apply strong security configuration settings to the online account. o Many types of online accounts, especially those of high value, often have additional security options that can be configured. An example can be that the sites will text a security confirmation code to your mobile phone to authorize transactions.	Medium

Network Access Points (Wi-Fi and Similar)

If any of your network access points are not secure, they can be accessed relatively easily. What constitutes a secure standard is evolving, however the most basic steps for connection points are:

Security Control	Security Level
o Change the default access password that any router, firewall or Wi-Fi device is shipped with.	Standard
o On Wi-Fi devices, select a secure connection protocol, such as WPA2. This is not unbreakable but is more resilient than other standards such as WEP. o A WEP connection can be broken into in under a minute by any reasonably capable amateur.	Standard

o Avoid networking home and small business devices wherever possible.
    o Setting up fully trusted relationships between devices is a technique that is rapidly dying out. That is because 'trusted' networks can spread cyber attack malware from device to device very rapidly.
    o If each of your devices is separately secure and only shares information through secure platforms, any cyber attack can often be limited to a single device rather than everything.
    o For example, central storage can still be achieved using a secure online service, without the need to establish direct security trust between every device.
	Standard

Security Control	Security Level
Similar solutions exist to coordinate, manage and control device security.	

o Update the firmware regularly.
   o Just like other devices, your network items (router, firewall, Wi-Fi access points) all run programs that the manufacturer offers updates for from time to time.
   o Usually those updates are to address vulnerabilities and improve security.
	Medium

o On Wi-Fi devices, do not broadcast the **SSID**. You should also change the name of the SSID from its default as it is usually set to a name that is based on the manufacturer (LINKSYS or NETGEAR). A default SSID name (even if not broadcast) is still easy to find.
   o The SSID is the name that appears when you scan for available networks to connect to.
   o The importance of this control will depend on where you live and what you leave connected to the internet.
   o Taking these steps makes it harder for any local opportunists to find your Wi-Fi connection. You can still connect your devices – but you have to know the SSID name instead of scanning for it.
   o Without this control, it is pretty easy for people to steal the use of your internet access.
	Medium

o Set a long and complex Wi-Fi access password. o The longer the length of the password, the less susceptible it will be to potential intrusion. Some people go to extreme lengths, with literally tens of characters as this password is only required when setting up a Wi-Fi connection for a new device.	Medium
o Make sure you have a securely configured network **firewall** in place. o If you want to secure what goes on within your home or small business network, you need a fire-	Medium

Security Control	Security Level
wall to create a barrier between the internet and what happens inside your local network. ○ A firewall works by applying rules to what data connections can enter and exit your local network. ○ Advanced firewalls also have additional features that can help to mask your location (**NAT** or 'Network Address Translation') and detect or even block some types of potentially malicious activity (network **IDPS** or 'intrusion detection and prevention system').	High
○ Upgrade your router security software to a higher standard. ○ There are alternative router security software options available for more advanced users who would like to apply higher levels of security.	High

Note: Every device has a unique **MAC address** (unique identifier) and it is possible to configure network devices to only accept specifically authorized MAC codes. However, there is continual debate about the effort versus protection this technique provides. This is because MAC addresses can be easily spoofed (faked).

For that reason, I have not included MAC address registration and filtering as an explicit basic form of defense. It can, however, be useful in very high security environments.

Email & Messaging

NOTE: Email and messaging are by their nature insecure. Once you send a message out to a recipient – you usually have no control over security at the receiving end or who the recipient may send the communication on to.

Emails often become an unofficial repository of your most valued and sensitive information and can frequently be used to transact sensitive information.

Keep these points in mind. It is easy to become complacent about email systems because they are used day-to-day for low value transactions too.

Security Control	Security Level
o Enable anti-spam and junk mail filters on your email services and device security software.	Standard
o Only disclose email addresses publicly that you do not mind receiving SPAM and malware attempts to. 　o It is worth having more than one email account; one for secure usage and one for low security usage. 　o Make the low security email account one that you can re-direct (forward to a different address). That way – if you do end up receiving large amounts of spam or malware attempts you can steer them away from any device you would like to keep clean and secure. o Use your low security email as your contact address for any unknown sites and accounts where you have to use an email address but do not fully trust the security.	
o Do not use your email as a storage archive. Store any valuable content to a secure storage device and keep the information stored in an offline archive if it is not required to be actively available. 　o Email is a leading method for attackers to get sensitive information about their victim. 　o The most secure email processes remove email after 90 days or less.	Medium
o If you need to send confidential or high value information over email, make sure the content is placed in an encrypted zip file with an unguessable secret key. 　o Never send the secret key with the same email. 　o If possible, only send the secret decryption key for the file via a separate route, such as a text message to the known mobile (cell) phone number of the recipient.	High

Locally Connected Hardware (Printers and similar)

Security Control	Security Level

o   Make sure the security configuration of any locally connected hardware is set to an appropriate standard.
    o   If the device is accessible over a local network or via any form of wireless or remote access, it can potentially be subject to unauthorized access.   For example, you can find that your printer can be sent print jobs that were not from you.
    o   Usually, a secure configuration means changing or disabling any default account passwords that are provided as standard with the item.
	Standard

Internet of Things Devices

Security Control	Security Level
o Remove any default accounts and passwords. o Remember, especially if your internet of things device, such as a home thermostat or CCTV is designed to be accessible remotely, it could be compromised (subject to unauthorized access and control) if you do not set high security options or if you leave default usernames and passwords in place.	Standard
o Keep software patches up to date. o Even smart device manufacturers find holes or new vulnerabilities in their operating systems. Update the software whenever the manufacturer offers one.	Standard
o Read the manufacturers security instructions and follow them.	Standard

Security Control	Security Level

o Keep access restricted to locations where you need it.
 	
   o Although your smart device may have some fun capabilities to enable access when you are away from the home or office, that same capability will then open a greater potential for the device to be compromised remotely. Only enable these remote access features when you need them.
 	
   o Take all the security configuration steps that are recommended by the manufacturer, especially those relating to enabling remote access.
	High

Disposal of Devices & Electronic Information

Security Control	Security Level

o Before you dispose or re-sell any device – be extremely careful to remove any information of value. This should include removing locally stored files and any usernames and accounts held in the device itself, for example – if you have a Twitter or other app that already has your password authenticated – remove it or change your password!
 	
   o Remember – just hitting the DELETE key alone does not really get rid of information. Even a factory reset leaves data accessible on the storage device for people who know what they are doing.
 	
   o You can run a specialist deletion routine. Tools to do this can be found. Look for something that runs a 'DoD level wipe' – one that meets the US Department of Defense standards for data removal. Prices start from free.
	Standard
	
	Medium

Security Control	Security Level
○ Retaining records beyond their useful life is actually considered a bad practice. Many of the most embarrassing losses of information related to files that were so old, they had little to no value. ○ For key records such as email, financial records and – for small businesses - priority operational records – define how long they should be kept for – and have a process to get rid of them at the end of their useful life.	Medium

Keep in mind that security threats are constantly changing. Additional security processes and technologies will be required.

What is contained here are most of the basic security techniques that can be applied to substantially reduce your risk of cyber attack and help you recover in the event you have one or more device compromised.

One of the easiest security measures we can all take is to use different devices for different purposes (low value and high value activities).

For example, you should always avoid dubious online behaviors, such as surfing to unknown sites. However, if for research or other reasons you find that activity necessary, look to do it from a 'junk' device that contains nothing of value and is not connected to your higher value devices.

Chapter 5: Summary of Key Points:

- The security controls applied to each device, account and process should reflect its risk value:
  - Standard (as a minimum)
  - Medium (as defined in Chapter 2)
  - High (as defined in Chapter 2)
- Security should be applied to:
  - Devices with operating systems
  - Additional options for mobile devices
  - USB storage and local network storage devices
  - Online accounts and password management
  - Network access points (Wi-Fi and similar)
  - Email & messaging
  - Locally connected hardware (printers, etc)
  - Internet of Things devices
  - Disposal of devices and information

6: Combating Phishing & Vishing

During the process of writing this book, I was updating and amending account details in a payment system. A notification email arrived in the inbox of my high security machine, appearing to be from the payment service.

It looked very authentic and asked me to click on the link to verify my recent actions. Some sites do send emails like this – but no secure site will ever send you a link and ask you to re-enter username or password details.

I forwarded the email across to my junk device (the one with no data of value on it and no connection to any other device).

From the junk device, I clicked on the link and it took me to a very convincing looking screen asking me to confirm my username and password.

The second that I got to the site, I knew this was a scam because it was an email link to a screen asking for log-in details. However, that could easily already have been too late. I had already clicked on the link. If there was malware at the site, my machine would already be infected.

Fortunately, 2 things saved me:

1) This was a simple scam that was only looking to persuade me to part with my password. I didn't fall for that part.
2) I used a 'junk' machine to access it. That machine has no information of value. That meant that even if there had been malware, I would not have been compromised.

What is important to understand is that no matter how vigilant you think you might be, or how security aware, it is still really easy to be caught out by scams.

'Click here to unsubscribe' to that irritating site that appeared to email you and you could find that it was a clever attempt to load in malware.

Remember – **no legitimate provider ever asks you to reveal your password via any email link, phone** or in any other way.

These scam emails will look like they link to the legitimate site – **never use an email link to get to a log-in page** – any provider that asks you to do this is following a poor security practice.

Some organizations now have incredibly sophisticated levels of cyber threat defense. As the number of threats increased, so have the number of security technologies to detect, prevent, remove and investigate attempts.

Despite all of these measures, even in the most robust and secure environments, some attacks still get through.

No matter how much security you put in place, there is one weakness or vulnerability that is always present. Ultimately, there always need to be some people who have to have legitimate access.

If you can leverage or steal a real persons authorized access, then you can bypass nearly all those layers of security.

For these reasons, most cyber attacks have a ***social engineering*** aspect. What I mean by that is that most cyber attacks try to break in by persuading YOU, the legitimate user to grant the attacker an access route. For example:

- That you should open a document or other file on the web or in a message that looks harmless but in fact contains malicious software.
- That you should click on a malicious link to view or action something from a message, website or even a physical letter, when that action would in fact be opening up your device to the attackers' malicious software.
- That you should disclose some personal information over the phone to someone who pretends to be from a legitimate organization. This technique often uses some information they already have to help convince the person of their authenticity. (We know your name and phone number and need you to confirm your password, bank details, account numbers, …)

The main ploys used by criminals are known as ***phishing*** and ***vishing***.

Let's briefly look at those definitions again, followed by some examples. Then finally we can look at what these scams have in common.

phishing – *using an electronic communication (for example email or instant messaging) that pretends to come from a legitimate source, in an attempt to get sensitive information (for example a password or credit card number) from the recipient or install* **malware** *to their device. The methods of phishing have evolved so that the message can simply contain a link to an internet location where malware is situated or include an attachment (such as a PDF or Word document) that installs malware when opened. The malware can then be* *used to run any number of unauthorized functions, including stealing information from the device, replicating further malware to other accessible locations, sharing the user screen and logging keyboard entries made by the user. Less complex forms of phishing can encourage the recipient to visit a fake but convincing version of a website and disclose password or other details.*

vishing *– abbreviation for **voice ph**ish**ing**. The use of a phone call or similar communication method (such as instant messaging) where the caller attempts to deceive the recipient in to performing an action (such as visiting a URL), or revealing information that can then be used to obtain unauthorized access to systems or accounts. Usually the ultimate purpose is to steal (or hold ransom) something of value. These types of calls are becoming extremely regular, as the criminal gangs involved may have stolen part of the recipients data already (name, phone number, …) to help persuade the person receiving the call that it is authentic. As a rule, if you did not initiate a call or message, you should never comply with any demand, especially to visit any webpage or link.*

Last week I got a **vishing** call.

The caller (I could hear the call center noise) said he was from a security site that I subscribe to (in fact I don't subscribe to that site). He said that he had found several of my devices were infected and that he was phoning to help me out

Really?

He gave me the name of the company and encouraged me to visit the URL to confirm it. Of course, that would have been the scam. The second I pressed return on the URL, the malware would be loading in and starting to lock me out from my computer. He could then pretend that this was the threat he was calling about and offer to unlock the ransomware for a fee.

Before my mother passed away, she was lucky enough to receive a physical letter informing her that she had won money on the Spanish Lottery. 'Mom. Did you even play the Spanish Lottery?' Of course not – but if she just went online and entered some information – then the inference was that the money would be hers.

Avoiding Phishing and Vishing is all about education and awareness. Not just your own but also for anyone in your family or business that uses yours (or their own) devices.

Get them to read this chapter – but also remember to keep tuned in to the press for the latest scams and ploys.

It is worth installing safe surfing security software into any browsers you use to surf the internet. These have settings that can restrict you to tested and safe locations. At a minimum, they can block you from accidentally visiting links that are known to have unsafe content.

You will find that most scams involve recognizable components:

- If you are being pressured to do something quickly, the chances are it is part of a scam designed to harm you rather than help.
- If the offer is too good to be true, the chances are it is a scam to get you to open some document or link.
- If the letter, call, email or other message was unsolicited (it arrived un-invited) it may well be an attempt at a scam.

Don't fall for pressure tactics, or reveal information, even if a caller has some of your authentic information.

In 2016, a UK company called Talk Talk had partial information from some of their customers stolen. This included their names and phone numbers. The cyber criminals were soon calling some of those people, pretending to represent Talk Talk and get them to visit their malware.

This is an example of how even the disclosure of basic information (name, phone number and the name of a company they are registered with) can be used to mount cyber attacks.

A further and frequently used vishing ploy is to be asked to call the caller back using the legitimate number. The caller then pretends to hang up. When you think you are re-dialing, the original caller is still actually connected and uses this to convince you of their authenticity.

There is also a form of attack known as **smishing**.

smishing – a phishing attack that uses the simple message service (SMS) to send a malicious link or file to a phone as a text message. If the malicious link or attachment is opened, the device may be compromised. This form of attack can also use the MMS (multi media service).

Educate yourself and users of your devices.

There are now so many new forms of malware being created each day that even the best security software can only deal with a percentage of the threats. The best defense is to avoid attempting to click on a dangerous link or open any infected file in the first place.

Never open links or files from messages you did not initiate or from untrusted sources or disclose information to unsolicited callers – regardless of how they arrive.

Never reveal your password to anyone.

Never write down your passwords.

Do not use passwords that are easy to guess or break.

Always use separate and complex passwords for every high value account that you use. One of the first tactics used by a cyber criminal if they get a single username and password is to re-use that password in other high value accounts.

Chapter 6: Summary of Key Points:

- Most cyber attacks take place by getting a legitimate user to perform an action, open an attachment, click on a link or reveal information.
- Attacks can come from messages, emails, phone calls, letters and other techniques.
- Tactics that use pressure or 'too good to be true' offers are frequently used. Consider these behaviors as warning flags that indicate the caller or sender is attempting to get you to perform an action that will compromise your device or an online account.
- Never write down your passwords.
- Never reveal or share any of your passwords with anybody.
- Use different, complex and secure passwords for each different account you use.

Remember – the reason that people are targeted in these attacks is because it allows the cyber criminal to easily bypass other security measures by taking advantage of your legitimate access.

7: **Detect:** Recognizing if You Are Compromised

Modern cyber attacks often do not reveal themselves early on. Even very large organizations are frequently compromised for years before they discover the intrusion.

If large companies with high security budgets are struggling to identify when they have intrusions, you can imagine that for the usual home user or small business, the problem is even greater.

Some forms of cyber attack may not seek to directly harm you but just use part of your device and it's bandwidth to attack others.

Other times, there could be malware present that aims to sit quietly in the background as it captures keyboard entries or slowly steals a copy of the information that is on your device.

There are also very rapid and immediate techniques that look to lock you out of your own device or some of your information in return for a ransom payment.

Even with very sophisticated security software in place, due to the sheer number of new malicious software programs created every day (over 500,000), your security software may also be oblivious to the problem.

> *Note that even though anti-malware may only detect and protect less than 50% of threats, it still forms a vital part of reducing your cyber attack risk exposure.*

The main form of detecting threats as early as possible relies on 3 basic techniques:

1) Have as much good security software as possible installed to alert you to any known threats.

2) Ensure anyone who has access to your device is encouraged to let you (or for a small business – your lead security contact) know if they think they may have clicked on a link or opened an attachment that they subsequently believe may have been infected.

3) Look for any ***indicators of compromise***.

Cybersecurity: Home and Small Business

In this case, we are using the term indicators of compromise to mean that we are looking for any obvious and unusual patterns or behaviors that suggest somebody has unauthorized access to a device or account.

Here are some of the indicators of compromise that may be observed, even by the regular user:

- Substantial and consistent slowdown in the processing speed of one or more devices.
- Frequent hard drive activity or network traffic when there is nothing expected to be processing.
- Frequent device crashes.
- A failure to be able to install operating system updates.
- Uninvited pop-up screens, especially when not in any browser session.
- Extended boot or shut down time without any discernible reason.
- Unexpected outbound traffic exchanges (sometimes observable through network traffic monitoring lights such as on an internet router.)
- Uninvited changes to the web browser home page, or a browser opening up pages or links that were not selected.
- Any warning that your security software has been disabled.
- Indications that an account has been logged into when it was not by any authorized person.
- Any alert about running out of storage capacity when there should be plenty
- And the all time classic – finding out from people that they appear to be getting odd messages from you (that you did not intentionally send).

Even one of these symptoms is not a good sign; if you have multiple symptoms, there is a high chance that the device where this behavior is observed has malware on it.

Keep in mind that there are grades of malware. Some items are irritating and some are dangerous to your information. None are desirable.

Be aware that any device that you believe is infected has the potential to spread its problems on to other devices it gets connected to – and that includes any USB storage device.

My recommendation is to get any device exhibiting these symptoms cleaned and restored as early as possible.

If you do not choose to clean and restore the device, then at a minimum you need to keep the device contained (not able to communicate with others). Ideally, switch the device off and leave it off. It will likely be hunting for opportunities to spread the infection when switched on.

If you must switch it on, switch off your other devices and do not connect the infected device to any other device you want to keep clear of being compromised. Disable all communications settings on the device you believe is infected, such as Wi-Fi and Bluetooth.

As a general rule, it is considered that malware infections and other cyber attacks cost less to resolve the earlier they are detected and fixed.

You can find information on how to recover from a cyber attack in Chapter 10: 'How to Recover from a Cyber Attack'.

Chapter 7: Summary of Key Points:

- Anti-malware will detect some but not all cyber attacks.
- There are a large number of other indicators, including:
    - Frequent, unexpected hard drive or network activity.
    - Pop-up messages appearing outside of web sessions.
    - Friends reporting they are receiving odd messages from you.
    - Any alert that your security software is not working.
    - Frequent crashes.
    - Failure to be able to install automatic updates.
    - …
- Switch off any infected device and refer to the chapter on recovering from a cyber attack.

Keep any device suspected of being infected contained as soon as possible. (That means preventing it from being able to communicate with others). Ideally, switch the device off and leave it off. It will likely be hunting for opportunities to spread the infection when switched on.

As a general rule, it is considered that malware infections and other cyber attacks cost less to resolve the earlier they are detected and fixed.

8: Taking Small Business Cybersecurity Further

You may be surprised to know that most organizations that suffer substantial attacks usually turn out to have gaps in security that you could drive a fleet of trucks through. (That is the subject of my next book!)

However, for small companies, even a relatively small attack can have devastating consequences, especially if it causes major disruption to your cash flow or customer relationships.

What we will cover in this chapter are some simple, practical and relatively low cost steps that can increase your small business' ability to survive an attack.

For very small businesses, the main components are really:

- Document at least a basic cybersecurity plan
- Apply reasonable security everywhere.
- Educate your users with acceptable use guidance.
- Have an easy method to restore critical files, devices and systems within timelines that are acceptable to your business.
- Evaluate the risks involved each time you decide to add any new device or software. Add these to your plan, together with any additional security controls required.

We will shortly take a deeper look into each of the items above.

How far you then choose to take your small business cybersecurity should depend on 3 primary factors:

1) How sensitive your business activity and reputation is to a cyber attack.
2) How many electronic information records of value you store and transact.
3) How many employees and digital devices your company operates.

Achieving a higher standard of security is best supported by taking a known, organized, consistent and appropriate approach to your cyber threats and risks. This should be proportionate to the 3 factors directly above.

Documenting the basic components of your security can provide peace of mind to your own business and provide a baseline that you can improve on over time. It can also be used to help demonstrate to your customers that you take security seriously.

Generally (but not always), a company with less than 20 people and a limited number of small customers can survive without documenting their security policies, provided they have a capable security person in their ranks. In this scenario, you may have competent security practices but it may not be economical to pay to get everything documented.

However, if your small company expects to deal with highly sensitive information (perhaps you are a law firm), or if you have large organizations as customers; you will be expected to demonstrate that your security is appropriate to the information you deal with.

It is also possible to get very extreme cybersecurity in place, even for small companies, including technologies such as installing **Data Loss Prevention** software. However, there is a cost and you can find out more about that at the very end of this chapter.

*data loss prevention (DLP) – this term can describe both (i) technologies and (ii) the strategies used to help stop information from being taken out of an organization without the appropriate authorization. Software technologies can use heuristics (patterns that fit within certain rules), to recognize, alert and/ or block data extraction activities on **digital devices**. For example, to prohibit specific types of file attachments to be sent out via internet mail services. They can also prevent or monitor many other attempts at removing or copying data. There are workarounds that can be used by skilled hackers that can evade detection by these solutions, including encryption and fragmentation. Although these solutions are becoming an essential line of defense, the most secure environments aim to prevent any significant set of data being available for export in the first place. For this reason, data loss prevention is often thought of as the last line of defense (a final safety net if all other security controls have not been successful). **Information loss prevention (ILP)** is an alternative version of the same term.*

Create a Cybersecurity Plan

In fact, we have covered many of the components that would be documented into a cybersecurity plan already within this book.

An effective cybersecurity plan can be a short document of only a few pages where you just ensure that you list out all the right steps and processes, then follow them.

If you think of our 4 step model – we can use that to create 4 sections in our Cybersecurity Plan:

1) Identify
2) Protect
3) Detect
4) Recover

Identify:

Assets

This requires creating a basic list of your primary (high value) information assets and the systems you use to process them. This process is covered in Chapter 2 of this book.

Remember to specifically identify the business risk value level against each asset (high, medium or standard) based on the confidentiality, integrity and availability you have assigned.

You would also identify what device types are used to process or manage that information. The risk value of any device should be based on the highest risk value of the information it accesses or stores.

Based on the **Identify** information, when you get to the **Protect** section, you will be applying security measures appropriate to the value of the information.

You will need to review and re-evaluate the risks involved each time you decide to add any new device type or software of business significance. Any significant new device type or software you choose to adopt will need to be added to your cybersecurity plan.

Even if you do not add new software or device types, you should review your full plan regularly and update it. I recommend this happens at least once every 6 months, given the speed at which the threats are now changing.

Threats

If you have any business specific cyber threats, these should also be identified. For example, if you hold any credit card data in your own systems or high value intellectual property, you might reasonably expect to be a greater target for cyber attacks designed to steal information.

If your business has a critical dependency on continual access to its information (for example – an accountancy company) – you might expect to be more targeted for a **ransomware** attack.

A ransomware attack can be overcome without payment to the attacker, if you have safe access to backup information and the ability to quickly recover or switch devices.

The main cyber threat used on small businesses is a cyber attack that uses **ransomware**. As covered earlier in the book, this type of malware intentionally locks you out of some (or all) of your critical information and then demands money in return for unlocking that information.

This type of attack is often used on small companies, as the price of unlocking the information is often perceived to be a small fraction of the cost of the potential business disruption and damage that would be caused by having the information remain locked.

My strong advice is never to pay a ransomware demand. Provided you have kept frequent and up to date secure backups of information, you will be able to restore your information.

Conversely, if you choose to pay a ransomware demand, you are likely to be placed on a 'sucker list' and repeatedly targeted by cyber criminals.

The purpose of the **Identify** section of the plan, is to encourage your business (during the **Protect, Detect** and **Recover** stages) to focus on having defenses and processes appropriate to the resilience level you need to address these attacks.

Protect:

Chapter 5 lays out many of the basic security measures that can be applied to your security approach. This section would document what primary security steps you will apply. You can use a framework similar to chapter 5 and should adjust (edit or add) further controls based on your specific business security needs.

- **Staff onboarding, security training and offboarding.**
- Devices with operating systems
- Additional measures for mobile devices
- USB storage and local network storage devices
- Online accounts and password management
- Network access points (Wi-Fi and similar)
- Email & messaging
- Locally connected hardware (printers, etc)
- Internet of Things devices
- Disposal of devices and electronic information

NOTE: There is an additional topic above (bold text) as it is worth having consistent processes when issuing or removing access. Security training (some key tips to include in security training can be found in chapter 6) should be given to all new joiners and at least annually to everyone.

Remember to swiftly remove access to devices and accounts whenever an employee leaves.

You should also educate users on what you consider to be the **acceptable use** of your small business devices and systems. It can help and is usual in large companies to get the employee to sign that they have read, understand and agree to the acceptable use policy. This can define items including whether your business devices can be used for private webmail, social media usage, internet shopping and so forth.

acceptable use policy – *a set of wording to define an agreement between any user and the enterprise that owns the service, application or device being accessed. The agreement would usually define both the primary permitted and prohibited activities.*

Remember that insider threats, either from accidental misuse or from the intentional actions from disgruntled employees, happen frequently.

Within any employee security training, do not forget to provide clear instruction on how they should report any known or suspected security problem. This will also be covered in the Detect section of your plan.

Privileged access to systems, such as the ability to install new software, should be restricted. Any new software installed should be thoroughly checked to ensure that it is secure before it is implemented, especially if it is from an un-known software house.

If in doubt, the security of new software can be researched online and tested in an isolated machine.

Detect:

In this part of the plan you will outline how security attacks would be detected and what the reporting process is. If there is any known or suspected security problem – who should be alerted and what should the reporter do?

Your security software may alert you.

You can also choose to educate your staff on the indicators of compromise listed in Chapter 7.

Not all security problems are of equal severity. When a problem is detected, you will want the recipient to assess the magnitude of the problem and then apply the appropriate action.

You should also outline how you will grade the security problem. One way to do this is to consider if the detected issue can impact:

- No significant operations (low severity)
- Some less critical operations (standard severity)
- A critical operation (high severity)
- All critical operations (critical severity)

When you get to documenting the Recovery approach, you can then assign a response or resolution time based on the severity.

Recover:

This section of your plan will show that you have documented your recovery process. It will show that your recovery process includes:

1. Confirming if the security issue is real.
2. Containing the problem.
3. Identifying the cause.
4. Restoring the operations and devices affected.
5. Reviewing if the recovery process was effective.
6. Applying any additional security or process changes that can prevent the problem from re-occurring.

Chapter 10 will cover the main steps required to restore devices after any attack in more detail.

The key part to being able to recover is to make sure that you have safe, secure and regular backups of your critical information. This ensures that your small business has the ability to quickly restore operations in the event of an attack.

Based on the severity level of any security incident or problem, you should also identify how rapidly you would require steps 1 through 4 to complete.

Remember that your planned recovery time needs to reflect (be shorter than) the time your business can operate without the affected software or devices being available.

Additional Small Business Security

There are additional and advisable security measures that a small business can implement.

It would also be accurate to state that security exists on a curve, up to a certain point it helps protect your organization from threats and disruption. Beyond a certain point, it can cause more disruption than it prevents.

Poorly configured and managed security software can create more business disruption than it prevents. For example, I saw a company installing a very advanced cyber defense (a technology known as deep level content inspection) that has the possibility to block transmission of any chain of data it's administrators require. That's great if it is run effectively – but in the early deployment design, nobody thought to consider how either a single bad rule (block everything with the letter 'a') or a compromise of the administration console could bring down the entire business.

At the device level, ***mobile device management*** solutions for laptops, tablets and smart phones can allow you to configure what software is acceptable, track where a device is when it is connected, restrict certain functions and even remotely wipe the information it contains.

Installing device level ***data loss prevention*** (DLP) can alert and block the movement of certain types of information based on rules that can be configured. This can help to alert and identify both intentional user actions and hidden attempts by malware to move data, even the movement of information onto USB devices.

The next chapter outlines the measures you can apply at the network level. This includes items such as advanced network firewalls.

However, my recommendation is that if you are a small business, it may actually be advisable to avoid having a traditional network that allows devices to 'trust' each other.

If your devices and platforms are independently secure and configured to run and report their security status to a central business security solution, you will have less chance of any cyber attack shutting down all of your operations.

There is more about this technique in the next chapter.

As a small business, you should also consider having a contingency plan if you have reliance on any commercial or cloud solution that could itself suffer from a cyber attack. Although major platforms tend to have very advanced security, that also makes them a frequent target. What can you do if that cloud accountancy package were to be unavailable for a few days?

Just like an individual, you should choose your software and cloud service providers carefully, based on the level of security and reliability they offer. Most of these providers can be excellent, provided you configure the security appropriately and have a contingency plan. The contingency plan is essentially a mini **Business Continuity Plan**, to be able to continue operating if the normal service for something critical to your business becomes unavailable.

There are also other security measures that can be applied to the information itself. We have already looked at making sure devices have **encryption**. Remember that high value information should be encrypted whenever it is sent or received (not only when it is at rest on a storage device). An example of this was provided earlier, locking information into an encrypted zip file with a secret password before it is sent. (The password should then be sent by a separate method such as a phone text message to the intended recipient).

Taken together, these processes help to ensure that risks are reduced because they will get your company to manage key security processes and practices in a consistent way.

In my experience of reviewing the security at all sizes of organizations (from Silicon Valley start-ups and basement companies to Amazon Web Services), the larger the company, the more essential it is to have solid (but lean and efficient) security practices that are documented and followed.

If you operate a larger company, or manage the delivery of online services, you will need to go further with your security than the basic tips outlined in this book. Items such as a full *security architecture* and a holistic approach to *identity and access management* are some of the essential components for larger organizations than this book was designed for.

In summary, if you are brilliant on the security basics outlined in this book, your chances of being compromised by an attack will be much lower. If you are attacked, you should have the ability to minimize the impact and swiftly restore any affected devices.

You will not be immune from attack, you will simply be far less likely to fall victim to them and more capable at minimizing the cost and disruption when they do occur.

Chapter 8: Summary of Key Points:

- To apply security consistently in any business requires putting together and following a Cybersecurity Plan.
- The four main sections in a cybersecurity plan include:
    - **Identify** (your valuable assets)
    - **Protect** (define your appropriate security steps)
    - **Detect** (find and report any compromised asset)
    - **Recover** (replace or restore any compromised asset)
- Start by identifying assets that present the highest risk to you.
    - Sets of high-value electronic files
    - Valuable online accounts
    - Items that damage you if stolen or unavailable.
- Only perform high value tasks on secure devices & connections.

Remember to swiftly remove access to devices and accounts whenever an employee leaves.

Be sure to set-up acceptable use and security training for all employees. Make sure that training is refreshed regularly (at least once each year).

Backups (copies) of important information should be stored in a secure location away from your main network and devices.

When you are ready to retire or re-sell any electronic device, be very sure to fully remove and destroy any sensitive information it contains. A factory reset, or pressing 'delete' does not usually destroy the information. Specialist software is usually required.

9: Sustaining Secure Devices & Networks

Having a local **network** of 'trusted' devices is a concept that is rapidly being consigned to the history books.

Even for large organizations, 'secure' network zones often have to exist in highly monitored, highly segmented environments, with very restricted access and extreme numbers of security precautions. Some data centers have zones like this.

The main networks in most organizations, are now subject to repeated infections. They are often far from secure. Cyber criminals and other threat actors all know that the easiest way to defeat security is by finding and leveraging someone with valid access.

The main problem with networks, especially for small businesses, is that they can create a **single point of failure**. What this means is that they can provide the potential for a single, successful attack to takedown your entire operation.

The reason for this:

- Networks build 'trust' relationships between devices.
- Devices can no longer defend against all threats.
- If one device in a trust relationship is compromised, there is a very high likelihood that some or all of the others will also.

We will be looking at the basic methods that can be used to help defend networks – however:

Keep in mind that running a network in the current climate is becoming a high risk / low reward method, especially for small business.

Households and small businesses that can work with a number of separate, securely built devices that collaborate over secure cloud software and are joined into a central, cloud security management solution will often find they have better security and resilience than those that operate on trust in a traditional local network.

If you do operate any kind of network, it is essential to be careful not to accidentally open any kind of insecure back door. Earlier in the book we mentioned the **internet of things**. As the number of devices we have that connect to the internet increases, homes will be more vulnerable to attack.

> *Any network is only really as secure as the weakest device that is given permission to connect to it.*

Brand new technologies and devices usually have security weaknesses at first. They present new opportunities to cyber criminals.

It is easy to open up a hole in a network that is intended to be secure, by simply connecting a trusted device with network access to an untrusted device.

If that untrusted device has an internet connection of its own, then a backdoor (an alternative way in) will be in place that can bypass all the security measures I have at the front door.

> *To maintain high security, never connect a trusted device to an untrusted device.*

For example: A new smart thermostat is allowed to directly connect to a smart phone and also to other devices intended to be secure in a home network. Separately, that same smart thermostat might have its own mobile data internet connection. If that is the case, connecting devices to the thermostat has created a potential route for my main network security to be bypassed.

Securing Networks

In addition to the basic steps outlined in Chapter 5, there are further technologies and steps that can be taken to secure a network, if you choose to have one.

Although this list will be useful, most of the steps are extremely difficult for the average person to do. It will usually be more secure and appropriate to define what you need, research it and agree an implementation price with a reputable and capable local network expert.

NOTE: Some network security devices may offer **unified threat management**. This can allow several of the measures below to be implemented on a network using a single device. As an example, it is possible to have a network level firewall, intrusion prevention, gateway anti-virus, gateway spam filtering and other functions all provided from a single device. This can be more practical, especially for sophisticated home network users and small businesses.

> *Servers on the network should follow the appropriate controls in Chapter 5.*

If you run application servers inside your domain, you will need to separately research the appropriate controls, as they will vary too much based on the software function and network design requirements to be covered in this book.

Security Control	Security Level

o   Install and configure a **network firewall** device at the network perimeter. This is a standard requirement if you do allow devices within the network to trust each other.
    o   The purpose of a firewall is to establish rules that restrict what electronic information is permitted to flow in and out of the boundary between the network you aim to keep secure and what it is connected to. For homes and small businesses that is usually the internet.
    o   You will need someone knowledgeable to set-up a **firewall** device. As you will see below, there is quite a lot to setting a firewall up securely and correctly.
    o   The basic principles for good firewall management are (i) for everything to be blocked by default (ii) the rules that are put in place that do permit traffic across the network threshold should be as specific as they can be – so that only genuinely required routes through the firewall will be usable – and that there are as few permitted routes as possible (iii) if the source location for a rule is not the general internet, the specific address (**IP address**) of valid locations that are permitted to communicate can also be configured (iv) the permitted destination IP address must be configured (v) the destination **port** also needs to be specified (vi) values of 'any' should always be avoided.
    o   The network address translation (**NAT**) filter function should be on a secure setting.
    o   NEVER FORGET to remove or change out any default administrative password.
    o   Using a firewall with a proxy function (a **proxy firewall**) provides the ability to further increase se-
	Standard

Security Control	Security Level
curity. A proxy service intercepts communications between devices inside the network and outside the firewall. It essentially breaks and reflects the information so that devices inside and outside of the network are only talking to the firewall and never directly to each other. The benefit is that this function can help to hide what is in your network from attackers. The drawbacks include that they are difficult to configure without expert help and slow down your information traffic.	Medium
o Do not rely solely on network security, look to maintain as much additional security on the individual devices as possible.	Standard
o Be sure that all the network security devices are maintained on the latest versions of software or firmware from their manufacturer.	Standard

o Implement a security solution across all devices that reports status and alerts to a central point.
  o The best security solutions can support a wide range of devices, including smart phones, tablets, laptops and others.
  o Alerts, including known malware intrusions and rogue activities (such as operating systems not updating or visits to unauthorized websites) can then be easier to identify and even notified as soon as they occur.
  o This can also detect issues when a device roams outside of the network, so that network access can be withdrawn until the device is made safe.
	Standard

o Restrict the network to known devices.
  o Do not permit unknown devices to be attached to the network or attached to items that are attached to the network.
  o If some form of guest access is occasionally required, this is more safely achieved by having a
	Standard
	
	Medium

Security Control	Security Level
separate or virtual network put in place, completely isolated from your secure network. o Every smart phone, laptop, tablet and other device with the ability to network is equipped with a unique identity known as a MAC address. It is possible to configure your network router to a restricted list of those addresses. However, it should be noted that these addresses can easily be scanned and spoofed (falsified), so security experts constantly debate the value vs. effort of this control.	
o Implement network level Intrusion Prevention. o This can be implemented as part of a unified threat management device, as a separate device or as software within a network server. o This will identify any patterns of network communication that are known or suspected to be associated with an intrusion. o Settings allow suspected threats to be logged, reported or blocked. It should be noted that blocking can sometimes disrupt legitimate traffic if the data transaction is mistaken for a potential threat.	Medium
o If you need to allow remote connection to the network from devices that are away from the main location, or connect 2 networks at different locations – make sure that a well configured VPN (virtual private network) can be used. This creates an encrypted tunnel between the remote location and the network. o Further security can be applied to any devices that roam outside the network, so that the VPN cannot be accessed through the device without additional verification that the correct user has the device. This is known as two factor authentication (needing more than the device alone).	Medium
o Have your network security scanned and tested. o There are various services at different price points	High

Security Control	Security Level
that can provide checks and reports on how robust your network security is. This will also provide advice on what actions can be taken to improve the security further.	
o Very high security devices should be restricted to their own separate network. Having more than one network (also known as network segmentation) allows you to better protect some assets and allow lower security standards and devices to operate in another. o This is a standard practice in larger organizations but is not always practical for home or small businesses.	High

These network security measures are not exhaustive and only represent the most fundamental steps and technologies in use. There are further security technologies that can be researched and implemented.

Securing the Internet of Things

There is a significant expected increase in the amount of internet connected devices around the home environment. Almost anything within an electronic circuit, from your smoke detector to your light bulbs, tv, fridge and even CCTV has options to be internet connected. Often they can also be remotely accessed and controlled.

To support these innovations, new, lower cost data networks are being established. This will soon allow these devices to maintain a constant connection. Most of these devices are also connected to our more trusted devices.

From a cyber criminals' perspective, we are creating a new and large **attack surface**, full of new weaknesses and potential opportunities.

Many of us will be adopting these devices. It is essential to consider the risks involved whenever you choose to start using a new device.

Points to consider should include:

- Does the device capture information that could be used against you? For example, a CCTV system, if connected to the internet and compromised can show if you are at home, who comes around, what your patterns are. Even a thermostat can indicate when you are away and not using your home.

- Will the device be sharing its information back with the manufacturer or any other organization? Many devices are priced low because of the additional value they can provide to their supplier due to the additional information they can collect. Even a smart tv can record conversations into text and indicate how often it is used and what it is used to watch.

- Will the device be required to connect to other devices of higher value? Connecting everything to your smart phone gives you visibility and control, but it also provides new security risks and opportunities for that control to be taken over.

- What would be the cost and impact if the device is compromised? Will it matter? If so how could I overcome that problem? As an example, if I get a ransom demand to be able to re-gain control over my own thermostat, what would that impact be?

Connected devices can be a lot of fun. The key message is to always consider the flip side (the risks).

One of the most interesting discussions in the security world on self-driving cars is this:

- How they can be secured against criminals actually managing to get vehicles to essentially steal themselves. After all, if an owner or customer needs valid access to order their vehicle to a location to pick them up, what prevents someone stealing that access and that high value asset.

Enjoy the new devices – but just take care to consider the risks and what they will be sharing and connecting to. If the risk is too high and the security is too low, it may be worthwhile waiting.

If you decide to have a hyper-connected set of trusted devices in your home or small business, you have opted to have a network and will need to look to apply network security measures.

For example, perhaps your self-driving car should only trust (take instruction or updates from) your secure device that will only be allowed to connect to it through a ***virtual private network***. Even then you would almost certainly want a second method of authentication to verify that the instructions have definitely come from you and not just your device.

Chapter 9: Summary of Key Points:

- Network of trusted devices should be avoided if possible.
  - o Trusted devices can more easily spread infections.
- Where a network is required, install network security:
  - o Network Firewall
  - o Use security software that centrally alert status issues.
  - o Network Intrusion Prevention
  - o ...
- Be sure to continue to maintain effective security on devices, do not rely on the network security alone.
- If two networks require a secure connection, use a **VPN** (virtual private network) connection.
- Get any high value network security tested for issues.
  - o Rectify any significant security gaps identified.

Any network is only as secure as the weakest device that is given permission to connect to it.

*NOTE: Some network security devices may offer **unified threat management**. This can allow several of the measures below to be implemented on a network using a single device. As an example, it is possible to have a network level firewall, intrusion prevention, network anti-virus, email spam filtering and other functions all provided from a single device. This can be more practical, especially for sophisticated home network users and small businesses.*

Households and small businesses that can work with a number of separate, securely built devices that collaborate over secure cloud software and are joined into a central, cloud security management solution will often find they have better security and resilience than those that operate on trust in traditional networks.

Carefully consider the value, security and risks before connecting any internet of things device to other devices.

To maintain high security, never connect a trusted device to an untrusted device.

10: Recovering from a Cybersecurity Attack

Recovery is no longer just a theoretical process that we might need.

The high volume of attack attempts mean many of us find ourselves restoring devices regularly.

Very often, a friend will ask me what they can do <u>after</u> some significant security problem has hit their critical device and information. If they have prepared (have anticipated this recovery process and have a safe and uncorrupted back-up copy of their critical information) – the recovery process is achievable.

The ability to recover is highly dependent on having access to a *safe and secure* backup copy of the information you need, when you need it. That means a copy of the information that does not contain the same security issue that is affecting the devices or software that needs to be restored.

If you have not prepared, the recovery process is much harder, more costly and sometimes could mean that some or all of the information may not be safely retrievable.

Backup a separate copy of your important information regularly.

Keep the backup information safe, secure and separate from the master information it is protecting.

Recovery, even for a home or small business user, essentially requires the same steps:

1. Confirming if the security issue is real.
2. Containing the problem.
3. Identifying the cause.
4. Restoring the operations and devices affected.
5. Reviewing if the recovery process was effective.
6. Applying any additional security or process changes that can prevent the problem from re-occurring.

Due to the wide range of device types, applications and operating systems that may need to be recovered, this chapter focuses on the basic objectives for each step. It is only possible to cover the objectives of what needs to happen.

Cybersecurity: Home and Small Business

The specific 'how' each objective is achieved, especially during the **restore** step, will vary depending on the device and will need to be separately researched. This is because the process has literally millions of variations that are possible.

1. Confirming if the security issue is real:

One of the biggest challenges is determining *if* we have something to fix and whether the effort to fix the issue outweighs the damage or disruption it is likely to cause.

Sometimes, identifying that the security issue is real may be very straightforward. Examples can be:

- Your security software has alerted you to a known threat.
- You have been locked out of some or all information and have received a *ransomware* demand.
- You have so many indicators of compromise (see chapter 7) that you have no doubt your device is compromised.

In the cases above you can move directly to the next step. You will need to take further action.

In other cases, you may not be able to absolutely confirm that one or more security issues are definitely present. Perhaps someone did something that *may* have compromised a device or account but there are no immediate *indicators of compromise* (see chapter 7). In those cases, you will need to make a judgment call.

To be absolutely sure, you can chose to restore (essentially reset and recover the affected devices) and move through to the next step. If your device, or the information it accesses is high value, this approach is advisable.

Many security threats try and intentionally cover their tracks and show no indications. Even large companies with expensive security capabilities can have the same security threats present for several years without being able to identify that they are present.

Recovery takes effort. You will need to balance the risk of judging if the likelihood that a problem is present is so low that no further action is required, against the potential impact if you turn out to be wrong.

The safest route is always to restore any device you suspect has been compromised and move to the next step.

If you are leaning towards taking no further action, you can also look to engage in some further security checks before making a final decision whether to proceed.

You could choose to add or run additional and different security software on your device to help look more deeply for potential threats. Make sure that any security software is always from a trusted and known source.

You can also research the circumstances that took place to identify if what happened or what is happening is a known security issue that will create problems if not rectified.

2. Containing the problem:

At this stage, you have decided that there *is* enough of a known or a suspected security issue to need to take corrective action.

Anytime the device suspected of having security issues is connected to anything else, it has the potential to spread the security issue it has.

The first thing to do is to switch off the device completely. This is to prevent it from spreading the issue it has, or sending out any further data (electronic information) it might be stealing.

If switching the device off completely is not practical, you would instead need to fully disable all the connections it has (wireless, wired, Bluetooth, mobile network and so on). You should also remove all USB connected devices. Some of those USB connected devices may also be compromised, especially if they can store data.

You will need to repeat this containment process on all devices that are suspected to have the security issue.

What you are doing is something in security called ***decapitation***, preventing any compromised device from being able to communicate, receive instruction, send information or spread to other devices.

If it is an online account that has been compromised, notify the service provider and immediately change your account password from a safe (clean and secure) device. The service provider should be able to assist with the further action steps you need to take.

3. Identify the Cause:

Unless the cause of the problem is understood, we might go through the recovery process and find ourselves with the same problem either still in place or re-occurring soon after the restoration processes are run.

The objective here is to understand what happened to acquire the security issue in the first place, so that you can prevent it from re-occurring.

This is known as identifying the root cause. That is – to identify the initial action that created the security problem.

Was it when a particular USB key was plugged in? Did it start when a certain email link was clicked on?

Before moving to the next step, put whatever measures you can in place to prevent the security issue from repeating.

For example, if it was due to installing a certain piece of new software, do not re-install it. If it was due to opening a particular document or file, do not re-install or open that file.

4. Restoring the operations and devices infected.

Depending on your level of technical ability and the sophistication of the security issue, you may decide you need help with this step.

Remember if you have used a device suspected to be compromised, you should change the passwords on all accounts (even online services) that it has been used to access.

The usual process for restoring a device is:

- Re-build the compromised device back to its initial state through a factory reset process or similar. Be warned **this will delete the data that the device has on it**. If you have information on the device that was not backed-up, you may need to seek expert help first – and even then the data may not be safely recoverable.
- Make sure that you install your security software back on the device as a first step after the reset.
- Update the device with all operating system and security software updates.

- Check the basic device functions are showing no signs that the security issue has remained.
    - If the security issue has remained, switch off the device and seek expert help. Any device that still has the security issue after reset has had the intrusion take place in a part of the device storage (usually the master boot record) that will need more involved recovery from an expert. If the device is old or cheap, you may decide it is more economic to start over with a new device.
- On your clean, symptom free device, you should now re-install the software you need. Remember to also update all those applications with the latest software updates too.
- Find the last backup that you did that you are confident is uninfected. This is sometimes referred to as the 'last known good' copy of the information.
- Re-check that the security issues have gone. If the device was fine after reset but has failed after your backup information was restored, that will indicate that your back up data may contain a copy of the security issue.
- If the device is now clean and free from issues, complete any final configuration required to re-establish connections.

If you have critical devices that you cannot afford to be without for even short amount of times, you can optionally choose to have a similar spare device that can be used during the time it takes to get your primary device restored. For example, you could keep your old smart phone cleaned and ready, so that you can start to use that during the time that the usual device is being restored.

5. Review if the recovery was effective

Any time that you test or run a recovery process, think about anything that went wrong. This serves two purposes:

If any symptoms of a security issue have remained, it will allow you to identify what caused that security problem to remain and adjust the recovery process accordingly.

This can also help identify practical steps to improve the process in future.

If any symptoms of a security issue have remained, you will need to go back to step 1 – but this time with an improved plan of action.

6. Applying the lessons learned

It is usual during the recovery process to identify changes or additional security measures to introduce to help reduce the likelihood of the issue happening again.

For example, some of the most common obstacles to successful and effective recovery are found to be:

- The backup information was also infected.
  - o The most frequent failure to be able to recover information is because the only copy of the information is beyond retrieval on another device that is also infected.
  - o Most critical of all is to make sure you keep your backup information secure and separate from the devices whose information they are protecting. If your backup device and main device are on the same network, there is a reasonable chance that both could be affected in the event of an attack.
- The information was not backed up regularly enough.
  - o Make sure that you make safe, secure and regular backups of any information you value. The frequency of backup should reflect how much information you can afford to lose in the event of an attack.
  - o If you could easily recover after losing a weeks' worth of data, then you could choose to backup just once per week. If you could only recover if you lost a days' worth of data, you would backup each day.
- That the amount of time to perform the recovery was much too long.
  - o There are ways to speed up the recovery process by (i) testing the recovery process regularly (ii) having a spare device to use as the primary device (or devices) are restored or even (iii) having a different contingency plan for how to operate if your usual devices are down.

If you want recovery to be quick and smooth, you have to regularly test your recovery processes.

I tend to look to re-build and restore my personal devices at least once every 18 months. That ensures that all my account details and backups are kept well. This process forces me to think about anything of value that I was not backing up regularly.

Alternate where you backup your information to, or backup to two locations. This will mean that if one backup location is compromised, another should not be.

Remember that the key components to smooth recovery are:

- Have a recovery process for your priority devices.
- Test the recovery process regularly.
- Make sure you backup a copy of your important information away from the devices regularly and using a method that will not spread any infection to all copies of your backup data.

Chapter 10: Summary of Key Points:

- The key to recovery is to be prepared and perform regular backups of your important information.
- Recover consists of a 6 stage process:
  - Confirming if the security issue is real.
  - Containing the problem.
  - Identifying the cause.
  - Restoring the operations and devices affected.
  - Reviewing if the recovery process was effective.
  - Applying any additional security or process changes that can prevent the problem from re-occurring.
- Test your recovery process regularly.

Backup a separate copy of your important information regularly.

Keep the backup information safe, secure and separate from the master information it is protecting.

Remember if you have used a device suspected to be compromised, you should change the passwords on all accounts (even online services) that it has been used to access.

If you want recovery to be quick and smooth, you have to regularly test your recovery processes.

Alternate where you backup your information, or backup to two locations. This will mean that if one backup location is compromised, another should not be.

11: **Advanced Persistent Threats**

All cyber attacks share one common objective; power. The perpetrator wants to seek power over something of yours in order to gain financial or political gain.

The earlier in any attack that it can be stopped, the less cost and damage it is likely to cause you.

For a cyber attack to cause as much intrusion and benefit for the attacker as possible, it will often to seek to persist (remain) in an environment for as long as possible. This is called maximizing the **dwell time**.

For those of you interested in the more advanced techniques employed by cyber attacks, this chapter provides an overview of a technique known as **advanced persistent threats** or APTs.

advanced persistent threats (APTs) – a term used to describe the tenacious and highly evolved set of tactics used by hackers to infiltrate **networks** through **digital devices** and then leave malicious software in place for as long as possible. The **cyber attack lifecycle** usually involves the attacker performing research & reconnaissance, preparing the most effective attack tools, getting an initial foothold into the network or target **digital landscape**, spreading the infection and adjusting the range of attack tools in place and then exploiting the position to maximum advantage. The purpose can be to steal, corrupt, extort and/or disrupt an organization for financial gain, brand damage or other political purposes. This form of sophisticated attack becomes harder and more costly to resolve, the further into the lifecycle the attackers are and the longer it has managed to already remain in place. A goal with this threat type, is for the intruder to remain (persist) undetected for as long as possible in order to maximize on the opportunities of the intrusion – for example to steal data over a long period of time. See also **kill-chain**.

Experienced cybersecurity experts expect sophisticated cyber attacks, especially on larger organizations, to intentionally hide for as long as possible in order to create the maximum benefit to the attacker.

Once the attacker has a foothold in one device on a **network**, it seeks to spread to other devices.

> **networks** – *the group name for a collection of devices, wiring and applications used to connect, carry, broadcast, monitor or safeguard data. Networks can be physical (use material assets such as wiring) or virtual (use applications to create associations and connections between devices or applications.) Usually the devices on a network will have some form of trusted permissions that allow them to pass and share packets of electronic information. This can be used as a route for any malicious software to spread.*

These types of advanced persistent attack can either be opportunistic (they happened to get in) or if intentional, they are more usually employed on high value targets.

The lifecycle for an intentional advanced persistent threat is frequently expressed as having the following stages:

1. Identify the target
2. Perform reconnaissance
3. Prepare the tools
4. Deploy the intrusion
5. Gain an initial foothold
6. Establish connection between the target and attacker
7. Strengthen the foothold (spread the intrusion)
8. Exfiltrate data (steal information)
9. Remain undetected / cover the tracks
10. Leverage the theft (sell the information or similar)

Unless your home or small business has a particular high value, the level of effort will make it unlikely that you may be specifically targeted. However, steps 5 through 10 can also occur simply because you accidentally got compromised by some malware.

When a person or organization is specifically targeted, the attacker will research them. That means gathering all the intelligence they can, from the internet and potentially even going as far as trying to get information from insiders (employees or knowledgeable suppliers). At the extreme, it has even been known for attackers to intentionally position someone inside the organization.

Even using only internet sources, quite a significant amount of information can usually be obtained. For example, applications such as Harvester can scrape public information from social media websites to pull together lists of employees, with their email addresses, job titles and so forth.

To be able to plant an initial intrusion, the attacker can easily design one or more customized pieces of malware. There are applications that exist that enable malware to be composed and uniquely encrypted with little to no technical expertise. In other words, a new form of malware can be created with about as much skill as it takes to put together a document or presentation.

There are many different ways for the attacker to get their malware into their target environment. They are techniques we have already covered but can include:

- ***Spear phishing*** – sending the malware in as an attachment or link using email addresses known to be inside the target organization.
- ***Social engineering*** – persuading a target known to have access to do something – such as visit a particular link or disclose a piece of information. Vishing (voice phishing) is sometimes used, calling a known employee number, pretending to be another employee, executive, supplier or customer that needs something done.
- ***Fake websites*** – perhaps with articles of particular interest to the target.
- ***Zero day*** exploits – leveraging a newly discovered security hole that has yet to have a repair issued.

Put in very simple terms, the attacker is seeking to find a weakness (cyber term '***vulnerability***') that they will subsequently ***exploit***. One of the most frequent types of vulnerability is to look for devices where the software, especially the operating system, has not been updated with the latest patches. The failure to update software will mean that there are known techniques the malware can use to bypass the usual defenses in that device.

Once the malware is in place, it will seek to find a way to communicate with the attacker. This is so it can receive instructions, report status and identify routes to send out the information it can steal. This is known as the attacker establishing command and control.

When seeking to eradicate these cyber threats, one of the first things we look to do is to make sure that the malware cannot send or receive information. Without this capability, the malware has no value to the attacker. It is for this reason that recovery starts with containing (isolating) infected devices.

The earlier in the lifecycle that the threat is caught, the cheaper it is to resolve and the less damage and theft it can achieve.

The ideal situation is that the threat is stopped before it ever has the opportunity to get an initial foothold. If malicious email can be filtered out before the user has the chance to open it, or if an attempt to reach an unsafe URL is blocked, the infection and subsequent intrusion can be stopped from ever happening in the first place.

In a similar way, if the first device to get infected is isolated before it can do any damage; this will again keep the recovery costs and damage minimal.

However, once the threat is in place, it is usual for it to immediately seek to install further malware both on the same device and any other items it can connect to. This can be a humble USB stick, the **master boot record** of the device, other device folders, or any devices in the same network of trust.

> *If you are an individual or small business who has not set-up a network of trusted permissions between devices, it is much harder for any successful attack on one device to infect and disrupt any other.*

> *Remember; making Bluetooth or other connections (including moving a USB stick from one infected device to another), or sending and opening an infected email can still transfer malware between devices.*

Because individuals and small businesses can have either very small networks or maybe no networks at all, the attackers will usually move more quickly to leverage or monetize their attack. However, dependent on who your attacker is, they may seek to 'persist' in your devices to optimize the attack value.

Due to the positive benefits of defeating an attack as early as possible in its lifecycle – this chain of events is sometimes referred to as the kill chain. This is because the earlier in the chain you can 'kill' off the attack, the lower the expected cost and damage experienced.

Once the malware is in place, it will usually seek to locate information of value and send a copy of that to the attacker via a secure route. Usually the stolen information will be collected through a location that is itself a victim of malware. This helps to prevent the attacker to be identified, even if the destination for the data is traced.

A persistent attack will usually aim to remain undiscovered. This is because remaining in place will maximize the amount of information that can be stolen over an extended period of time and from a larger number of devices.

However, it can sometimes be the case that the attack pattern will change. As an example, once the attacker knows it has reached a high level of overall control, it could seek to lock critical devices and information so that the attacker can demand a ransom.

As the speed that information can travel increases, it is likely that many cyber attack lifecycles will also accelerate. If someone wants to steal large amounts of information at present, the connection speed can still require that the data theft happens over an extended time period.

Even once the technical attack is complete (the theft has finished), the consequences can continue for some time. The monetary value for the attacker is about the separate resale, blackmail or ransom funds.

A great example of this was the theft of data from Linked In back in 2012, that went back on the market in 2016, creating a need for further actions by the victim.

Fortunately, cybersecurity is getting stronger all the time. The disciplines within a cybersecurity department in a country or large company are as diverse as they would be in the average hospital.

Unfortunately, the threats and techniques are also evolving. As new technologies are developed and deployed, the attackers are continually searching for the next weak point to emerge.

If you are interested in learning more about the discipline of cybersecurity and security testing techniques– the next recommended publication to read is **'Cybersecurity for Beginners'**.

Chapter 11: Summary of Key Points:

- Advanced Persistent Threats usually only intentionally pursue high value targets.
- The typical lifecycle is:
    1. Identify the target
    2. Perform reconnaissance
    3. Prepare the tools
    4. Deploy the intrusion
    5. Gain an initial foothold
    6. Establish connection between the target and attacker
    7. Strengthen the foothold (spread the intrusion)
    8. Exfiltrate data (steal information)
    9. Remain undetected / cover the tracks
    10. Leverage the theft (sell the information or similar)
- The earlier that the attack is discovered, contained and addressed, the lower the damage and cost is likely to be.

If you are an individual or small business who has not set-up a network of trusted permissions between devices, it is much harder for any successful attack on one device to infect and disrupt any other.

Remember; making Bluetooth or other connections (including moving a USB stick from one infected device to another), or sending and opening an infected email can still transfer malware between devices.

If you are interested in learning more about the discipline of cybersecurity – the next recommended publication to read is **'Cybersecurity for Beginners'**.

12: **Remember the Cybersecurity Basics**

The better your cybersecurity is, the more you will be able to safely do with your accounts and devices.

This section pulls together a small selection of some of the most basic and essential security steps from across the book:

Always install a good anti-malware software solution on each device.

Always delete any message or communication you receive that contains any links or attachments from an unknown source and never click on the links or open the attachments they contain. If you did not initiate the communication, the chances are very strong that any links or attachments will be an attempt to install malware.

Always keep your digital devices up to date with the latest software patches from the manufacturer, especially for the operating system.

Avoid using untrusted network connections (such as public Wi-Fi) and public locations to access any high value online accounts, such as payment systems and online banking.

If you receive an unsolicited call asking you to perform any kind of action or visit any kind of website. Do not be pushed into doing what they ask.

If you ever access an account you own and notice any online account activity that is suspicious, you should immediately take 2 steps:

1) Report the activity to the service provider.
2) Immediately change your password for that account.

*If you do find (or suspect) that you have a digital device that has been compromised, never perform an insecure transfer of files between the device and an uninfected device. For example, if you copy files on to a USB stick, that USB stick is then likely to have the same infection and will spread it if inserted or connected to another device. Refer to the chapter on '**Recovering from a Cyber Attack**'.*

For high risk, high value devices and online accounts, always use a separate and complex password. It is also worthwhile using a discrete and different username if this is possible (some usernames are unfortunately locked to being your email address).

Never re-use the same username and password combination on any accounts of value.

Never write down or reveal your password for any account.

*You can store a physical log of your username and passwords using '**The Encrypted Book of Passwords**' as this allows you to keep part of the information secret, so anyone accessing your book would still not be able to access the accounts, unless you reveal your secret keys.*

If you do want to access potentially harmful websites, or open potentially harmful attachments or links, do it on a device that you don't mind messing up! This is usually a cheap device that you can easily perform a factory reset on. Make sure you own the device, do not mess up other peoples devices. Also be aware that factory resets do not always get rid of malware.

Items with high risk to availability will require that you make frequent backups (copies) of the information into a separate location. The backup location should be somewhere secure and separate from the master information. That means taking a copy to somewhere that will not be compromised if your main devices and data are. This could be an encrypted USB key, or a secure cloud storage service. If you have a small business or home network, it is not advisable to keep backup copies of information only on your local network. If you do (and your network is compromised) you may otherwise still lose your backup information.

When you are ready to retire or re-sell any electronic device, be very sure to fully remove and destroy any sensitive information it contains. A factory reset, or pressing 'delete' does not usually destroy the information. Specialist software is usually required.

*The possibility of insiders creating either intentional or accidental exposure of your information can be reduced by restricting their access to the minimum they need. For example, not providing any unnecessary permissions to the user (for example - no **administrative access**) or to not allow them to access certain equipment or information.*

*Wherever practical, always keep the number of installed software applications to a minimum. That will help to keep your devices running faster and decrease the amount of **nagware**, **spyware** and **adware** you are exposed to. Uninstall software that you no longer need or use.*

Keep any device suspected of being infected contained as soon as possible. (That means preventing it from being able to communicate with others). Ideally, switch the device off and leave it off. It will likely be hunting for opportunities to spread the infection when switched on.

If you are an individual or small business who has not set-up a network of trusted permissions between devices, it is much harder for any successful attack on one device to infect and disrupt any other.

Households and small businesses that can work with a number of separate, securely built devices that collaborate over secure cloud software and are joined into a central, cloud security management solution will often find they have better security and resilience than those that operate on trust in traditional networks.

Carefully consider the value, security and risks for any internet of things device.

To maintain high security, never connect a trusted device to an untrusted device.

Remember if you have used a device suspected to be compromised, you should change the passwords on all accounts (even online services) that it has been used to access.

If you want recovery to be quick and smooth, you have to regularly test your recovery processes.

Alternate where you backup your information, or backup to two locations. This will mean that if one backup location is compromised, another should not be.

Remember; making Bluetooth or other connections (including moving a USB stick from one infected device to another), or sending and opening an infected email can still transfer malware between devices.

*If you are interested in learning more about the discipline of cybersecurity — the next recommended publication to read is '***Cybersecurity for Beginners***'.*

Cybersecurity to English

This section is an abridged version of the separate publication 'The **Cybersecurity to English Dictionary'**. It contains only key terms used in this book.

The full version of this dictionary is available as a separate publication.

acceptable use policy – *a set of wording to define an agreement between any user and the enterprise that owns the service, application or device being accessed. The agreement would usually define both the primary permitted and prohibited activities.*

administrative access – *any electronic account that has authority to allow elevated activities to be performed. An elevated activity is any that can apply significant changes to one or more **digital device**, software application or service. For example, the permission to install new software is considered an elevated privilege requiring this elevated authorization level.*

administrative permission – *the process of granting authority to a person so they can gain the type of elevated access known as **administrative access**. See **administrative access**.*

adware – *any computer program (software) designed to render adverts to an end user. This type of software can be considered a form of **malware** if (i) the advertising was not consented to by the user, (ii) is made difficult to uninstall or remove, or (iii) provides other covert malware functions.*

anti-malware – *is a computer program designed to look for specific files and behaviors (**signatures**) that indicate the presence or the attempted installation of malicious software. If or when detected, the program seeks to isolate the attack (quarantine or block the **malware**), remove it, if it can, and also alert appropriate people to the attempt or to their presence.*

anti-virus – *predecessor of **anti-malware** software that was used before the nature and types of malicious software had diversified. This is a computer program designed to look for the presence or installation of specific files. If or when detected, the program seeks to isolate the attack (quarantine or block the **virus**), remove it, if it can, and also alert appropriate people to the attempt. A virus is only one form of malware, so the term anti-malware is considered to be more inclusive of other forms of malicious software. However, as people are more familiar with the term 'anti-virus' this can sometimes be used to describe some types of anti-malware. See also **anti-malware** and **virus**.*

advanced persistent threats (APTs) *– a term used to describe the tenacious and highly evolved set of tactics used by hackers to infiltrate* **networks** *through* **digital devices** *and then leave malicious software in place for as long as possible. The* **cyber attack lifecycle** *usually involves the attacker performing research & reconnaissance, preparing the most effective attack tools, getting an initial foothold into the network or target* **digital landscape***, spreading the infection and adjusting the range of attack tools in place and then exploiting the position to maximum advantage. The purpose can be to steal, corrupt, extort and/or disrupt an organization for financial gain, brand damage or other political purposes. This form of sophisticated attack becomes harder and more costly to resolve, the further into the lifecycle the attackers are and the longer it has managed to already remain in place. A goal with this threat type, is for the intruder to remain (persist) undetected for as long as possible in order to maximize on the opportunities of the intrusion – for example to steal data over a long period of time. See also* **kill-chain***.*

attack surface *– the sum of the potential exposure area that could be used to gain unauthorized entry to, or extraction of information.*

backup *– (i) the process of archiving a copy of something so that it can be restored following a disruption. (ii) having a redundant (secondary) capability to continue a process, service or application if the primary capability is disrupted.*

Bluetooth *– a short range wireless standard for the connection of devices.*

botnet *– shortened version of ro****bot****ic* **net***work. A connected set of programs designed to operate together over a network (including the internet) to achieve specific purposes. The purpose can be good or bad. Some programs of this type are used to help support internet connections, malicious uses include taking over control of some or all of a computers functions to support large scale service attacks (see* **denial of service***). Botnets are sometimes referred to as a zombie army.*

Business Continuity Plan *– (abbreviation BCP) an operational document that describes how an organization can restore their critical products or services to their customers should a substantial event that causes disruption to normal operations occur.*

computer virus *– see* **virus**

cyber attack *– to take aggressive or hostile action by leveraging or targeting* **digital devices***. The intended damage is not limited to the digital (electronic) environment.*

cyber attack lifecycle *– a conceptual model of the sequential steps that are involved in a successful unauthorized intrusion or disruption into a* **digital landscape** *or* **digital device***. There are a number of models currently available, an example of the most common steps found across the models are illustrated within the definition of* **advanced persistent threat***. See also* **kill chain***.*

cyber criminal – *any person who attempts to gain unauthorized access to one or more* **digital device***.*

cybersecurity – *the protection of* **digital devices** *and their communication channels to keep them stable, dependable and reasonably safe from danger or threat. Usually the required protection level must be sufficient to prevent or address unauthorized access or intervention before it can lead to substantial personal, professional, organizational, financial and/or political harm.*

data loss prevention (DLP) – *this term can describe both (i) technologies and (ii) the strategies used to help stop information from being taken out of an organization without the appropriate authorization. Software technologies can use heuristics (patterns that fit within certain rules), to recognize, alert and/or block data extraction activities on digital devices. For example, to prohibit specific types of file attachments to be sent out via internet mail services. They can also prevent or monitor many other attempts at removing or copying data. There are workarounds that can be used by skilled hackers that can evade detection by these solutions, including encryption and fragmentation. Although these solutions are becoming an essential line of defense, the most secure environments aim to prevent any significant set of data being available for export in the first place. For this reason, data loss prevention is often thought of as the last line of defense (a final safety net if all other security controls have not been successful). Information loss prevention (ILP) is an alternative version of the same term.*

decapitation – *(in the context of* **malware***) preventing any compromised device from being able to communicate, receive instruction, send information or spread malware to other devices. This can effectively render many forms of malware ineffective because it removes any command, control or theft benefit. This is a stage during threat removal.*

Denial of Service (DoS) – *an attack designed to stop or disrupt people from using organizations systems. Usually a particular section of an enterprise is targeted, for example, a specific network, system, digital device type or function. Usually these attacks originate from, and are targeted at, devices accessible through the internet. If the attack is from multiple source locations, it is referred to as a distributed denial of service or DDoS attack.*

device encryption – *usually refers to encoding (making unreadable) the information at rest on a smart phone, tablet, laptop or other electronic item. This encoding makes the information stored on the item readable only when a valid user is logged in.*

digital device – *any electronic appliance that can create, modify, archive, retrieve or transmit information in an electronic format. Desktop computers, laptops, tablets, smart phones and internet connected home devices are all examples of* **digital devices***.*

digital landscape – *the collection of* **digital devices** *and electronic information that is visible or accessible from a particular location.*

dwell-time – *in the context of* **cybersecurity** *– how long an intrusion or threat has been allowed to remain in place before being discovered and eliminated.*

encryption *– the act of encoding messages so that if intercepted by an unauthorized party, they cannot be read unless the encoding mechanism can be deciphered.*

fake website — *can either be (i) a fraudulent imitation of a real internet page or site designed to look like one from the legitimate company or (ii) an internet page or site from a completely fake company, often with a 'too good to be true offer' or content. In both instances, the objectives for the pages can include, to capture real log-in credentials, to receive real payments for orders that will not be delivered or to install malware.*

firewall *– is hardware (physical device) or software (computer program) used to monitor and protect inbound and outbound data (electronic information). It achieves this by applying a set of rules. These physical devices or computer programs are usually deployed, at a minimum, at the perimeter of each network access point. Software firewalls can also be deployed on devices to add further security. The rules applied within a firewall are known as the firewall policy.*

hacktivism *– an amalgamation of hacker and activism. Describes the act of seeking unauthorized access into any digital device or digital landscape to promote a social or political agenda. Usually the unauthorized access is used to cause destruction, disruption and/or publicity. Individuals participating in these acts are called* **hacktivists**.

hacktivist *– an amalgamation of the words hacker and activist. Describes any individual who participates in* **hacktivism**.

IDAM *–* acronym for **Id**entify and **A**ccess **M**anagement *- the collection of processes and technologies used to manage, confirm, monitor and control legitimate access to systems by authorized accounts. This includes measures to ensure each access request is from a verified, expected and legitimate person or entity.*

IDPS *– see* **Intrusion Prevention System**.

indicators of compromise (IOC) *– is a term originally used in computer forensics to describe any observable behaviors and patterns (such as particular blocks of data, registry changes, IP address references) that strongly suggest a computer intrusion has or is taking place. The collation of these patterns and behaviors are now actively used in advanced threat defense to help more rapidly identify potential security issues from across a monitored digital landscape.*

Internet of Things (IoT) *– the incorporation of electronics into everyday items sufficient to allow them to network (communicate) with other network capable devices. For example, to include electronics in a home thermostat so that it can be operated and share information over a network connection to a smart phone or other network capable devices.*

Intrusion Prevention Systems (IPS) – *a computer program that monitors and inspects electronic communications that pass through it, with the purpose and ability (i) to detect, block and log (record key information) about any known malicious or otherwise unwanted streams of information and (ii) to log and raise alerts about any other traffic that is suspected (but not confirmed) to be of a similar nature. These programs are usually placed in the communication path to allow the prevention (dropping or blocking of packets) to occur, for example, within advanced firewalls. They can also clean some electronic data to remove any unwanted or undesirable packet components.*

internet protocol – *is the set of rules used to send or receive information from or to a location on a network, including information about the source, destination and route. Each electronic location (host) has a unique address (the* **IP address***) used to define the source and the destination.*

IP address – *see* **internet protocol.**

kill chain – *a conceptual cyber defense model that uses the structure of attack as a model to build a cyber defense strategy. The stages in an advanced persistent threat are typically used as a framework. The model works on the basis that the earlier in the lifecycle (kill chain) a threat is detected and defeated, the easier and lower the cost incurred to manage it.*

MAC address – *abbreviation for* **media access control address***. This is a unique identifier assigned to every single digital device with a network interface controller. If a device has multiple controllers, it may have multiple (unique) addresses, one for each controller. If the identifier (mac address) is assigned by the manufacturer, part of it will include the manufacturer's identification number. There are several format conventions in existence. The identifier is used in network (including internet) communications.*

malware – *shortened version of* **mal***icious soft***ware***. A disruptive, subversive or hostile program placed onto a* **digital device***. These types of programs are usually disguised or embedded in a file that looks initially harmless but is actually designed to compromise a device or network of devices. There are many types of malware;* **adware, botnets, computer viruses, ransomware, scareware, spyware, trojans** *and* **worms***, these are all examples of malware. Cyber criminals often use malware to mount cybersecurity attacks.*

man-in-the-middle – *the interception and relay by a third party of selected content between two legitimate parties, for the purpose of hijacking or adjusting an electronic transaction. For example, party 1 believes they have connected to their banking home page but is actually on an emulated screen offered by the intercepting attacker. As the log-in information is provided, the attacker can set-up a separate connection to the bank (party 2) and is able to respond to any challenge made by the bank by passing the same challenge back to the user (party 1). Once authorized in the transaction system, the attacker can now make transactions that have not been sanctioned by the user, without their immediate knowledge.*

master boot record – *the first sector on any electronic device that defines what operating system should be loaded when it is initialized or re-started.*

Mobile Device Management (MDM) – *a technology used for the security administration of mobile devices such as tablets and smart phones. Able (for example) to remotely wipe information from a mobile device and control what applications and functions are permitted to be installed or run.*

nagware – *a form of software that persistently reminds the user that they should do something even though they might not want to. This is not usually considered malicious software but it does exhibit some unwanted features, disrupting the flow of the users' interaction with their device. Nagware is often used as partial payment for some forms of software, especially free software.*

NAT – *acronym for **N**etwork **A**ddress **T**ranslation. This is a router protocol, typically used also in firewalls to change (translate) the **IP address** between network addresses inside and outside a network gateway.*

networks – *the group name for a collection of devices, wiring and applications used to connect, carry, broadcast, monitor or safeguard data. Networks can be physical (use material assets such as wiring) or virtual (use applications to create associations and connections between devices or applications.) Usually the devices on a network will have some form of trusted permissions that allow them to pass and share packets of electronic information. This can be used as a route for any malicious software to spread.*

NFC – *acronym for **N**ear **F**ield **C**ommunication. A method of extremely short range data communication that uses electromagnetic induction and usually operates by touching devices together or from a maximum range of up to 2 inches or 5 cm.*

persistence – *to seek continued existence in a situation despite opposition.*

phishing – *using an electronic communication (for example email or instant messaging) that pretends to come from a legitimate source, in an attempt to get sensitive information (for example a password or credit card number) from the recipient or install **malware** to their device. The methods of phishing have evolved so that the message can simply contain a link to an internet location where malware is situated or include an attachment (such as a PDF or Word document) that installs malware when opened. The malware can then be used to run any number of unauthorized functions, including stealing information from the device, replicating further malware to other accessible locations, sharing the user screen and logging keyboard entries made by the user. Less complex forms of phishing can encourage the recipient to visit a fake but convincing version of a website and disclose password or other details.*

port – *part of the techniques that help organize the diverse range of communications and services that can take place between electronic devices and computer programs. By assigning a* *specific value (a port number) when sending information, the receiver can know what type of information it should be and how to process it. This information can also be used by security devices such as* **firewalls** *to help allow or deny certain communication types.*

router *— a device used to define the path for data packets (electronic information) to follow when they flow between networks.*

scareware *— malicious software that is designed to persuade people into buying an antidote, usually masquerading as a commercial malware removal tool or anti-virus package, but in reality provided by the attacker.*

social engineering *— The act of constructing relationships, friendships or other human interactions for the purpose of getting the recipient to perform an action or reveal information. The action or information revealed has the hidden purpose to achieve a nefarious objective, such as acquiring intelligence about the security, location or vulnerability of assets or even gaining the persons trust to open an internet link or document that will result in a* **malware** *foothold being created.*

security architecture *— a model designed to specify the features and controls across a* **digital landscape** *that help it to prevent, detect and control any attempts at disruption or unauthorized access.*

signatures *— (in the context of cybersecurity) are the unique attributes, for example, file size, file extension, data usage patterns and method of operation, that identify a specific computer program. Traditional* **anti-malware** *and other security technologies can make use of this information to identify and manage some forms of rogue software or communications.*

single point (of) failure *— a vulnerability that is so significant, it can be used to create devastating disruption to an entire organization.*

smishing *— a phishing attack that uses the simple message service (SMS) to send a malicious link or file to a phone as a text message. If the malicious link or attachment is opened, the device may be compromised. This form of attack can also use the MMS (multi media service).*

spear phishing *— a more targeted from of* **phishing**. *This term describes the use of an electronic communication (for example email or instant messaging) that targets a particular person or group of people (for example employees at a location) and pretends to come from a legitimate source. In this case, the source may also pretend to be someone known and trusted to the recipient, in an attempt to get sensitive information (for example a password or credit card number).*

spyware *— a form of malware that covertly gathers and transmits information from the device it is installed on.*

SSID – *acronym for **S**ervice **S**et **Id**entifier. This is the set of up to 32 characters that are used to recognize a particular Wireless Local Area Network (WLAN) connection on Wi-Fi routers and other access points. A list of the values can be seen when any device scans for visible wireless connections.*

The Encrypted Book of Passwords – *Writing your passwords down is usually fraught with risks. This book helps you to store your passwords more securely in a format that you can read but others will find hard to break.*

threat actors – *an umbrella term to describe the collection of people and organizations that work to create **cyber attacks**. Examples of threat actors can include **cyber criminals**, **hacktivists** and nation states.*

trojan – *an application (software program) that appears to be harmless but actually conducts other unseen malicious and unauthorized activities.*

Unified Threat Management (UTM) – *a security device that integrates a large number of security technologies and services. For example, a single gateway device that includes proxy **firewall, intrusion prevention**, gateway **anti-malware** and **VPN** functions.*

URL – *acronym for **u**niform **r**esource **l**ocator. This is essentially the address (or path) where a particular destination can be found. For example, the main address for the Google website is the URL http://www.google.com*

virtual private network (VPN) – *a method of providing a secure connection between two or more points over a public (or unsecure) infrastructure, for example, to set-up a secure link between a remote company laptop in a hotel and the main company network.*

virus – *a form of **malware** that spreads by infecting (attaching itself to) other files and usually seeks opportunities to continue that pattern. Viruses are now less common than other forms of malware. Viruses were the main type of malware in very early computing. For that reason, people often refer to something as a virus when it is technically another form of malware.*

vishing – *abbreviation for **v**oice ph**ishing**. The use of a phone call or similar communication method (such as instant messaging) where the caller attempts to deceive the recipient in to performing an action (such as visiting a URL), or revealing information that can then be used to obtain unauthorized access to systems or accounts. Usually the ultimate purpose is to steal (or hold ransom) something of value. These types of calls are becoming extremely regular, as the criminal gangs involved may have stolen part of the recipients data already (name, phone number, …) to help persuade the person receiving the call that it is authentic. As a rule, if you did not initiate a call or message, you should never comply with any demand, especially to visit any webpage or link.*

VPN – *see* **virtual private network.**

VPN tunnel – *the secure communication route between two* VPN *connection points. See also* **virtual private network.**

worm – *a form of malicious software (malware) that seeks to find other locations that it can replicate to. This assists to both protect the malware from removal and increase the area of the* **attack surface** *that is compromised.*

zero-day attack – *refers to the very first time a new type of exploit or new piece of malware is discovered. At that point in time, none of the anti-virus, anti-malware or other defenses may be set-up to defend against the new form of exploit.*

Made in the USA
Lexington, KY
22 January 2018